# Vintage Crochet

30 specially commissioned patterns

Susan Cropper

photography by Kristin Perers

jacqui small

First published in 2007 by Jacqui Small,
7 Greenland Street, London NW1 0ND

ISBN-10: 1 903221 88 9
ISBN-13: 978 1 903221 88 4

A catalogue record for this book is available
from the British Library.

2009  2008  2007
10 9 8 7 6 5 4 3 2 1

Printed and bound in China

Publisher **Jacqui Small**
Art Director **Barbara Zuñiga**
Commissioning Editor **Zia Mattocks**
Pattern Checker **Hazel Williams**
Technical Editor **Katy Bevan**
Stylist **Emily Chalmers**
Production **Peter Colley**

# Contents

Introduction 6

Beautiful, Sumptuous Yarns 8

**Boho Babes 12**
Beautiful clothes for hippie chicks

**Nostalgic Home 50**
Modern-retro furnishings for timeless homes

**Lazy Summers 70**
Pretty accessories for outdoor living

**Gorgeous Gifts 92**
Perfect items to give away or keep

Techniques 120

Suppliers 138

Designers' Biographies 140

Acknowledgements 142

# Introduction

To me, 'vintage' evokes slightly wistful emotions, inspired by the delightful combination of character and charm that's enhanced by an object's past use. The word is imbued with something intangible – it conjures up cabins in the woods, canoes by a lake, cowslip-covered fields, swallows, and the moody light of early morning, twilight on snow, candles and fairy lights.

These are some of the things that have inspired the patterns in this book. In their individual styles, each contributing designer has created a modern take on 'vintage', which is also playful, cosy, beautiful and slightly quirky. Any one of these patterns would sit as happily in – or look as gorgeous on you in – a snowy mountain cabin as in a stylish city apartment. Colours, too, can evoke these feelings, so we have worked in a sensitive palette of duck-egg blue, mauve, burnt orange, moose brown, fig, pale peach and eau de nil.

When I first dreamed of opening my London shop, Loop, it was crucial to me that it should be a place full of charm and beauty – a warm and welcoming space where people could come to be inspired, as well as to browse, buy, talk and learn. As a knitter and self-confessed yarn junkie, I had found it frustrating that there was no shop in the city that reflected the exciting new developments taking place in the world of knitting and crochet. There was nowhere that sold anything but a very limited selection of the breathtaking array of yarns that are now available, and nowhere that offered practical workshops on all aspects of knitting and crochet, along with made-up clothes, homeware, and quirky toys and accessories created by the wealth of talented young designers that are working in fibre. So, this is what I set out to achieve with Loop. Above all, I wanted it to be a space where everything to do with knitting and crochet was available under one roof – from vintage buttons and useful and unusual haberdashery to a varied selection of yarns, patterns, books and workshops, as well as the finished work of some of the most creative independent designers and makers.

Now, two years later, the shelves are filled with yarns from around the world. There is such a wonderful variety being produced today, and we stock everything from the simplest basic natural yarn to the kookiest hand-dyed handspuns. My passion for fibre, texture and colour never seems to wane, and one thing that drives me is my wish to pass on this enthusiasm to others and inspire them to create

beautiful things. From the simplest crocheted scarf to the most elaborate garment or throw - it is all possible with the same basic tools: a crochet hook and a length of yarn (or ribbon, or strips of fabric knotted together, or anything else you may wish to experiment with). That's all you need to create these amazing things - and, really, how cool is that?

It has been such an honour for me, through Loop, to meet a host of creative young designers who have reclaimed this traditional craft and stamped it with their unique sense of style. Their work is an inspiration and a cause to celebrate. All of the designers who have contributed patterns to this book have a connection to Loop in one way or another. Some are designers or designer-makers, whose wonderful patterns, yarn or finished work we sell; others work in the shop or teach the classes. I have the most enormous respect for them all, and collaborating with them - both at Loop and in the making of this book - continues to be a joy.

Most of the patterns are fairly straightforward and require basic to intermediate crochet skills - ideal for beginner crocheters, who just need a little nudge to try out shaping or new stitches. Others, such as Kristeen Griffin-Grimes's 'Betty' Shrug (see pages 36-41) or Leigh Radford's exquisite Papillon Canopy (see pages 84-7), are quite challenging. Both of these will demand patience and dedication, but the results will be worth it - they are some of the things that have made us 'ooh' and 'aah' as the samples came in. There also other gorgeous items to wear - a dress, a wrap and a cardigan, for instance - and sweet accessories, such as a scarf, a headband and a corsage. For a cosy modern-retro home, there are pretty tablecloths, blankets and the loveliest breakfast set embellished with vintage buttons.

Each designer has written their pattern in their own style, but the directions are all clear and there are step-by-step instructions for the trickier techniques (see pages 120-37). Once you set your heart on making one of the patterns, I suggest you read it through before you begin, to get a feeling for what is involved, and refer to the techniques section if necessary. It's always a good idea to practise on a swatch to get to grips with the stitch and required tension. Keep the swatch to refer to later and start building up a personal swatch library.

I hope you will feel inclined to make the patterns your own, too, by experimenting with different yarns, colours and embellishments. Feel free to decorate items with beads, buttons, pompoms and ribbons, as well as more unusual trims, such as lace flowers, charms or strips of fabric.

Vintage Crochet is a little extension of Loop and those who make it special. We hope you love the patterns as much as we do and find some inspiration within these pages to make some pretty wonderful things for yourself and others. Happy crocheting!

# Beautiful, Sumptuous Yarns

I feel sure that the resurgence in popularity of knitting and crochet in recent years is partly due to people being seduced by the gorgeous variety of yarns that are now available. Who wouldn't be? Yarn shops today are as beautiful and enticing as cake shops! The luscious array of colours on offer - from mouthwatering hot pinks and oranges, rich berry purples and vibrant greens to the soft, subtle shades of dirty lilacs, chalky blues and muddy greys and browns - and the myriad textures - from the softest cashmere and fluffy angora, to smooth cotton and silk, to exquisite ribbon, sparkly yarn and nubbly handspuns - means that we are literally spoilt for choice.

Beautiful yarns are what inspired me to open Loop, and this small space, with its lovely outdoor deck and cosy fireplace, now brims with more than 130 different yarns from all over the British Isles, North and South America, Continental Europe, Australia, South Africa and Japan. Each has their own soul and character, from pear tree's speckled fine merino, which is so divine it feels like cashmere, to Blue Sky Alpacas Alpaca Silk, with its gorgeous saturated colours and beautiful drape, to the subdued palette of Debbie Bliss yarns and the wonderful hand-dyed Bamboo yarn from Be Sweet - the choice is astounding. There is truly a sense of joy in sourcing the most exquisite and unique yarns. When I go to yarn trade fairs in Europe or the United States, I could swoon with delight as I wander along the endless aisles of merinos, mohair, hand-dyes, handspuns, bouclés,

Left: There are many different textures of yarn available in gorgeous vintage hues, such as Blue Sky Alpacas 'Melange', a divine 100% baby alpaca yarn with a heathered look, in shade 812 Blue Cheese (top); Blue Sky Alpacas 'Alpaca Silk', 50% alpaca and 50% silk, in shade 136 Champagne (bottom left); and Lana Grossa 'Royal Tweed', 100% merino fine, in shade 32 (bottom right).

Opposite: An array of crochet hooks from Clover, Balene and Susan Bates. Vintage buttons are wonderful to collect and add instant character to a crocheted piece. As well as using them for fastenings, you can sew them on as an embellishment, along with velvet ribbon. These examples have been chosen to complement the rich colour of Blue Sky Aplacas 'Melange' in shade 807 Dijon.

tweeds, ribbons, chenilles, bamboo, cashmere, alpacas and silks. And I am always thrilled when I hear the exclamations of delight as people browse around the shop. It is a lovely moment, too, when a customer brings a new discovery into the shop to share with us – and sometimes those yarns will eventually end up on the shelves.

Yarn comes from animals (for example, sheep, rabbits, goats, alpacas and silkworms), plants, recycled fabric and synthetic materials. There is wool, merino, mohair, cashmere, alpaca, angora, silk, cotton, linen, hemp, paper, bamboo, acrylic, steel wrapped with silk, stainless-steel wire (which is particularly good for crocheted jewellery) and an endless variety of blends of these fibres available as yarn. Yarn from rare breeds, as well as handspun and hand-dyed, Fairtrade and organic yarns, are also growing in variety as well as accessibility. You can also experiment with tearing fabric into narrow strips and tying them together, then crocheting with the fabric 'yarn'. Bee Clinch's Picnic Blanket (on pages 72–5) is a delicious example of this. Vintage fabric or ribbon is great for this and works well as a lovely edging for a throw or blanket.

There are many different weights of yarn: lace-weight, 4-ply and double-knit (DK), Aran weight, chunky and super-chunky. In general, as long as it is a similar fibre, you can substitute one yarn for another if it has the same tension or 'gauge'. Make a swatch before you begin, though, as you may need to adjust your hook size.

There are many innovative independent yarn spinners and dyers producing unusual yarns and pushing the boundaries of what yarn can be. Among them are Gina Wilde, of Alchemy Yarns in California, who hand-paints silk, mohair and bamboo; Nadine Curtis, of Be Sweet, adding nubbiness, beads and ribbons to her delicious colours of hand-dyed yarns from South Africa; and Takako Ueki, of Habu, sourcing the most exquisite unusual yarns from small mills around Japan. There is also Lexi Boeger, of PluckyFluff, who handspins her yarn and throws in the most gorgeous combinations of felted flowers, beads, sequins, pompoms, buttons, cloth and bobbles.

Opposite: We've got stash! There are all kinds of yarns to choose from – including ggh 'Amelie', a manmade fibre that feels like angora, as well as cashmere, silk, alpaca, felted merino and ribbon yarns.

Right: Guv'nor, the dog, having fun messing around with ggh 'Bel Air', a lovely lightly felted Aran-weight merino yarn in shade 19.

Though much too fiddly to crochet anything substantial with, this type of yarn makes a great edging if worked with a large hook.

There has also been a great resurgence of people spinning and dyeing yarn in small cottage industries. The full list of people involved in these crafts is too long to mention here, but the wide range, excellent quality and sheer beauty of their yarn is an indication of the energy and excitement surrounding yarn today.

Whatever yarn you choose, always buy the best quality your budget allows. So much time goes into making the piece that your work deserves the best materials.

Boho Babes

D ramatic oversized crochet motifs in the softest merino and silk yarn create an open, airy wrap worthy of a glamorous Hollywood star. Inspired by the signature style of silver-screen legend Ava Gardner, the 'Ava' wrap is easily constructed in one piece in Louisa Harding's 'Grace' yarn. This is a great intermediate project that will bring vintage pizzazz to any outfit.

# 'Ava' Wrap

## Kristeen Griffin-Grimes for French Girl

### MATERIALS
Seven 50g balls Louisa Harding Grace, shade 04 Powder
5.5mm crochet hook
Tapestry needle

### MEASUREMENTS
**Finished size (blocked):** 50 x 200cm (20 x 80in).

### TENSION
One pattern repeat (18 sts) = 14.6cm (5¾in).

### ABBREVIATIONS
See page 120.

### WRAP
Make a slip knot, then ch 257 for foundation row.
**Row 1:** Tr 1 into 7th ch from hook * ch 1, miss 1 ch on foundation row, 1 tr in next ch, repeat from * to end. This will leave you with 253 sts to work the main pattern into.

#### Begin main pattern
**Row 2:** Ch 6, miss 3 sts, * 1 dtr in each of next 3 sts, ch 3, miss 3 sts, (1 dtr, ch 3, 1 dtr) in next st, ch 3, miss 3, 1 dtr in each of next 3 sts, ch 5, miss 5 sts, repeat from * to 3 sts before end, ending with ch 2 instead of ch 5, 1 dtr in last st. Turn.
**Row 3:** Ch 6, * 1 dtr in each of next 3 dtr from last row, ch 1, (1 dtr, ch 1) 7 times into ch-3 space, 1 dtr in each of next 3 dtr, ch 5, repeat from * to 3 sts before end, ending with ch 2 instead of ch 5, dtr in 4th ch of beginning ch-6 from row 2. Turn.
**Row 4:** Ch 5, * 1 dtr in each of next 3 dtr, ch 5, dc in ch st between

1st and 2nd tr, (ch 6, dc in next ch) 5 times, ch 5, 1 dtr in each of next 3 dtr, ch 3, repeat from * to 3 sts before end, ending with ch 1 instead of ch 3, place dtr in last st (4th ch in beginning ch-6 from row 3). Turn.

**Row 5:** Ch 4, * 1 dtr in each of next 3 dtr, ch 5, dc into 1st ch-6 from last row. Continue to (ch 6, dc into ch-6 from last row) 4 times, then ch 5, place 1 dtr in each of next dtr, ch 1, repeat from * to end, eliminating ch 1, miss 1 st, place 1 dtr into 4th ch in ch-5 from last row. Turn.

**Row 6:** Ch 4, place 1 dtr in each of next 3 dtr, * ch 5, dc into next ch-6 loop from last row. (Ch 6, dc into next ch-6 loop) 3 times, ch 5, place 1 dtr in next 2 dtr, dtr2tog over next 2 dtr, 1 dtr in each of next 2 dtr, repeat from * to 4 sts before end, ending with 1 dtr in next 2 dtr, dtr2tog over last 2 sts. Turn.

**Row 7:** Ch 4, place 2 dtr in each of next 2 dtr, * ch 6, dc into 1st ch-6 from last row. (Ch 6, dc in next ch-6) twice, ch 6, place 1 dtr in each of next 5 dtr, repeat from * to 3 sts before end, ending with 3 dtr in last 3 dtr. Turn.

**Row 8:** Ch 4, miss 1st dtr, place 1 dtr in each of next 2 dtr, * ch 7, dc into 1st ch-6 loop, ch 6, dc into next ch-6 loop, ch 7, place 1 dtr in next 5 dtr, repeat from * to 3 sts before end, ending with 3 dtr instead of 5 dtr. Turn.

**Row 9:** Ch 8, place 1 dtr in each of next 3 dtr, * ch 8, dc in ch-6 loop, ch 8, 1 dtr in next 2 dtr, then place (1 dtr, ch 5, 1 dtr) in next dtr, 1 dtr in each of next 2 dtr, repeat from * to 3 sts before end, ending with 1 dtr in next 2 dtr, then [1 dtr, ch 2, 1 trtr (wrap yrh 3 times)] in last st (4th ch in ch-4 from row 8). Turn.

**Row 10:** Ch 6, dtr into trtr from last row, ch 3, 1 dtr into each of next 3 dtr, * ch 7, place 1 dtr in each of next 3 sts, ch 3, place (1 dtr, ch-3, 1 dtr) in ch-5 loop, ch 3, place 1 dtr in each of next 3 sts, repeat from * to 3 sts before end, ending with ch 3, (1 dtr, ch 1, 1 trtr) in 6th ch in ch-8 from last row. Turn.

**Row 11:** Ch 5, (1 dtr, ch 1) 3 times into ch-1 from last row, * place 1 dtr in each of next 3 dtr, ch 5, place 1 dtr in each of next 3 dtr, ch 1, then (1 dtr, ch 1) 7 times into ch-3 space, 1 dtr in each of next 3 dtr, ch 5, repeat from * to 9 sts before end, ending with 1 dtr in each of last 3 dtr, ch 1, (1 dtr, ch 1) 3 times, 1 dtr into ch-6 loop from last row. Turn.

**Row 12:** Ch 7, dc in 1st ch-1 space, (ch 6, dc into ch-1 space) twice, ch 5, 1 dtr in each of next 3 dtr, ch 3, * place 1 dtr in each of next 3 dtr, ch 5, place dc in 1st ch st between 1st and 2nd tr, (ch 6, dc in next ch) 5 times, ch 5, 1 dtr in each of next 3 dtr, ch 3, repeat from *, ending with 1 dtr in each of the last 3 dtr, ch 5, dc in next ch-1 space, (ch 6, dc into ch-1 space) twice, ch 3, 1 dtr into 4th ch of ch-5 from last row. Turn.

**Row 13:** Ch 1, dc into the top of dtr from last row, ch 6, dc into ch-6 loop from last row, ch 6, dc into next ch-6 loop, ch 5, 1 dtr in each of next 3 dtr, ch 1, * 1 dtr in each of next 3 dtr, ch 5, (ch 6, dc into ch-6 loop from last row) 4 times, then ch 5, place 1 dtr in each of next dtr, ch 1, repeat from * to end, ending with 1 dtr in each of last 3 dtr, ch 5, dc, into ch-6 loop from last row, (ch 6, dc into ch-6 loop) twice. Turn.

**Row 14:** Ch 7, dc in 1st ch-6 loop, ch 6, dc in next ch-6 loop, ch 5, * place 1 dtr in next 2 dtr, then dtr2tog over next 2 dtr, 1 dtr in each of next 2 dtr * ch 5, dc into next ch-6 loop from last row, (ch 6, dc into next ch-6 loop) 3 times, ch 5, repeat from * to last 2 ch-6 loops from last row, ending with dc into 2nd-to-last ch-6 loop, ch 6, dc in next ch-6 loop, ch 3, 1 dtr into dc at beginning of last row. Turn.

**Row 15:** Ch 1, dc into the top of dtr from last row, ch 6, dc into ch-6 loop from last row, ch 6, * place 1 dtr in each of next 5 dtr, ch 6, dc into 1st ch-6 from last row, (ch 6, dc in next ch-6) twice, ch 6, repeat from * to last 2 loops, place (1 dc, ch 6, 1 dc) over last 2 loops. Turn.

**Row 16:** Ch 7, dc in ch-6 loop from last row, * ch 7, place 1 dtr in next 5 dtr, ch 7, dc into 1st ch-6 loop, ch 6, dc into next ch-6 loop, ch 7, place 1 dtr in next 5 dtr, repeat from * to last ch-6 loop, dc in ch-6 loop, ch 3, 1 dtr into dc from beginning of last row. Turn.

**Row 17:** Ch 1, dc into the top of dtr from last row, * ch 8, 1 dtr in next 2 dtr, then place (1 dtr, ch 5, 1 dtr) in next dtr, 1 dtr in next 2 dtr, ch 8, dc into top of ch-6 loop, repeat from * to last loop. Turn.

**Row 18:** Ch 12, * 1 dtr into each of next 3 dtr, ch 3, place (1 dtr, ch-3, 1 dtr) in ch-5 loop, ch 3, place 1 dtr in each of next 3 sts, ch 7, repeat from * to last ch 7 ending with long tr, with yarn wrapped around hook 5 times placed in dc from beginning of last row. Turn.

**Rows 19–23:** Repeat Rows 3–7.

### FINISHING

Weave in all ends using a tapestry needle.

Pin out and block lightly by spraying with water (see page 137).

This pretty shift dress is an adaptation of an original 1960s design. The bodice is worked in treble crochet and the skirt in panels of 'Irish' crochet motif. The two sections are connected by a treble eyelet row threaded with matching ribbon. The skirt can be made longer or shorter by either adding or reducing the number of panels in the skirt.

# 'Nico' Dress

## Bee Clinch

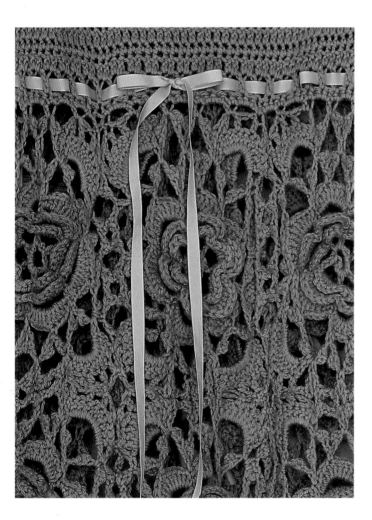

## MATERIALS
Ten 50g balls Debbie Bliss Cashmerino Aran, shade 05 Smoky Blue
5mm crochet hook
Tapestry needle
1m (1yd) matching satin ribbon, 1cm (½in) wide

## MEASUREMENTS
One-size dress fits sizes 10-14.
**Finished measurements:** bust 94cm (37in), length of back bodice 28cm (11in), length of skirt 58cm (23in).

## TENSION
Each motif measures 18 x 18cm (7 x 7in).
18 st to 10cm (4in) using a 5mm hook.

## ABBREVIATIONS
See page 120.

## NOTE
This dress is based on an orginal 1960s pattern, which comes in only one size; it can be worn either loose or close fitting and looks great both ways. Because it is made up of square motifs, the only way to size it up or down would be to add or reduce the number of motifs or panels in the skirt section.

## SKIRT
To work a motif (make 18 in total): using a 5mm hook make 8 ch, sl st to beginning to form a circle.
**Round 1:** 6 ch (counts as tr, 3 ch), * 1 tr into circle, 3 ch; repeat from * 4 times, sl st to 3rd ch of 6 ch (6 spaces).
**Round 2:** Into each sp work (1 dc, 1 htr, 3 tr, 1 htr, 1 dc) sl st to 1st dc (6 petals).
**Round 3:** * 5 ch, 1 dc into next tr of round 1, inserting hook into the back of the stitch; repeat from * ending sl st to back of 1st dc.
**Round 4:** Into each sp work (1 dc, 1 htr, 5 tr, 1 htr, 1 dc), sl st to back of 1st dc.
**Round 5:** * 7 ch, 1 dc into next dc on round 3 inserting hook into stitch from back; repeat from * ending sl st to back of 1st dc.
**Round 6:** Into each sp work (1 dc, 1 htr, 7 tr, 1 htr, 1 dc), sl st to 1st dc.
**Round 7:** 1 dc into 1st dc on next petal * 4 ch, 1 dc into 3rd ch from hook (picot made), 1 ch, 1 dc into centre tr of same petal (picot lp made), ** 4 ch, 1 dc into 3rd ch from hook; repeat from ** once, 1 ch, 1 dc into 1st dc on next petal; repeat from * omitting last dc and ending sl st into 1st dc.
**Round 8:** Sl st to centre of 1st picot lp (between picots), 1 dc into same lp, * 7 ch, 1 dc between picots on next picot lp, turn, 3 ch, 9 tr into 7-ch lp, 1 tr into next dc, 4 ch, turn, miss first 2 tr, 1 tr into next tr, ** 1 ch, miss 1 tr,

1 tr into next tr; repeat from ** twice more, 1 ch, miss 1 tr, 1 tr into top of 3 ch, 4 ch, 1 dc into 3rd ch from hook, 1 ch, 1 dc into same lp as dc after 7 ch, *** 4 ch, 1 dc into 3rd ch from hook, 4 ch, 1 dc into 3rd ch from hook, 1 ch, 1 dc between picots on next picot lp; repeat from *** once; repeat from * omitting last dc and ending sl st into 1st dc. Fasten off.

### Finishing skirt

Pin out each square, making the centre ch of the group the corner ch sp. Press lightly on the right side, leaving the centre 4 rounds unpressed (1st 2 rounds of petals).

Sew 9 squares together for front skirt (3 rows of 3 squares) and remaining 9 squares together for back skirt.

When sewing the squares together, use the picots and corner ch sps as joining points. The piece should still retain a lace-like appearance.

### FRONT BODICE

With right side of front skirt facing, using 5mm hook, rejoin yarn to corner ch and work as follows.

**1st foundation row:** 1 dc into corner ch sp * 3 ch, miss 1-ch sp, 1 dc into next ch sp, 3 ch, 1 dc into ch between the 2 picots, 3 ch, 1 dc into ch between next 2 picots, 3 ch, 1 dc into 4-ch lp, 3 ch, miss 1-ch sp, 1 dc into corner ch sp of worked motif and next motif; repeat from * across other 2 motifs, 1 ch, turn (15 ch sps).

**2nd foundation row:** 1 dc into 1st dc, * 3 dc into ch sp, 1 dc into next dc; repeat from * 6 times, (60 st), 2 ch, turn.

Now work in bodice pattern as follows.

**Row 1 (eyelet row):** 1 tr into 1st st, * 1 ch, miss 1 st, 1 tr into next st; repeat from * to end, 1 ch, turn.

**Row 2 (and subsequent even rows):** 1 dc into 1st st, dc to end, 2 ch, turn.

**Row 3 (and subsequent odd rows):** 1 tr into 1st st, tr to end, 1 ch, turn.

Work in patt until 14 rows in total have been worked (including eyelet row).

### Armhole shaping

**Row 1:** Sl st 3, 3 ch, tr to last 3 st, 1 ch, turn (54 st).

**Row 2:** Dc to end, 2 ch, turn.

Repeat 1st row of armhole shaping (48 st).

Continue in pattern with these stitches until 16 rows in total have been worked since start of armhole shaping, finishing with an even row.

### Left neck opening

Tr 12 st, ch 1, turn. Dc to end.

Continue with these sts for 6 more rows.

### Left shoulder shaping

**Row 1:** Sl st 6, ch 2, tr to end, 1 ch, turn.

**Row 2:** Dc to end. Fasten off.

### Right neck opening

With right side facing, rejoin yarn 12 st from right armhole edge, 2 ch, tr to end, 1 ch, turn.

Continue with pattern for 7 more rows.

Repeat left shoulder shaping but reversing instructions.

### BACK BODICE

Work as for front bodice, working 18 rows to neck shaping after armholes, finishing with even row.

### Left neck shaping

Work in pattern across 12 st, 1 ch, turn.

Work 3 rows without shaping.

Slope shoulder as given for front bodice.

Rejoin yarn for right side and work 3 rows; slope shoulder as for front bodice.

### SLEEVES (Make 2)

With 5mm hook ch 40 + 1.

**Row 1:** Starting in 2nd ch from hook, dc to end, ch 2, turn.

**Row 2:** Starting in 1st st, tr to end, ch 1, turn.

Repeat these 2 rows 3 times. Total 8 rows.

### Armhole shaping

**Row 1:** Sl st 3, ch 2, dc to last 3 st, ch 1, turn.

**Row 2:** Tr to end, 2 ch, turn.

**Rows 3–6:** Repeat these 2 rows twice (28 st).

**Row 7:** Sl st 1 at beg of next row, dc to 2nd st from end, 1 ch, turn (26 st).

**Row 8:** Tr to end, 2 ch, turn.

**Row 9:** Repeat last decrease row (24 st).

**Row 10:** Tr to end, 2 ch, turn.

### Upper sleeve shaping

**Row 11:** Sl st 6, dc to last 6 st, 1 ch, turn (12 st).

**Row 12:** Tr to end, 2 ch, turn.

**Row 13:** Sl st 3, dc to last 3 st, 1 ch, turn.

**Row 14:** Tr to end. Fasten off.

### FINISHING

Press bodice (see page 137).

All bodice seams can be joined with dc. Join shoulder seams.

With right sides together, insert sleeves into armhole arc.

Join side seams of motifs in the same way as described for joining skirt motifs. Join side seams of bodice.

Thread ribbon through eyelets.

Work 1 row of firm dc around neck, working 1 dc into each st or row end.

Crocheted in natural handspun organic cotton yarn, this 'flower-child' tunic reminds us of summer days, daisy chains and the sounds of buzzing bees and someone's radio playing in the distance.

# 'Joni' Flower Tunic    Bobbi IntVeld

## MATERIALS
Twelve (thirteen, fourteen, fifteen) 68g balls Blue Sky Alpacas
  Handspun Organic Cotton, shade 60 Natural Cream
3.75mm crochet hook
Tapestry needle

## MEASUREMENTS
**To fit four sizes:** S (M, L, XL).
**Bust:** 89 (99, 109, 119cm)/35, (39, 43, 47in).
**Length:** 64 (65, 66, 67cm)/25 (25½, 26, 26½in).
**Sleeve underarm:** 52 (52, 53, 53)cm/20½ (20½, 21, 21in).

## NOTE
Instructions for larger sizes are given in parentheses. Where there is only one figure, it applies to all sizes.

## TENSION
**Flower mesh pattern:** 10 sts, 5 spaces to 5cm (2in).
**Double crochet band:** 10 dc to 5cm (2in).
**Crossed treble crochet pattern:** 10 ctr to 5cm (2in).

## ABBREVIATIONS
See page 120.

## SPECIAL ABBREVIATIONS
**4lps - 4-looped puff stitch:** (Yrh, insert hook into st, yrh, draw up a loop pulling slightly to make an elongated st) repeat 4 times (9 loops), yrh pull though all loops, ch 1. (See also page 123).
**ctr - crossed treble:** Miss next st, tr into next st, tr into missed st. (See also page 124.)
**dc3tog:** Work 3 dc without pulling through the last st, and then pull a loop through all the loops on the hook.

## BACK
Ch 93 (113, 133, 153).
**Flower mesh pattern**
**Row 1 (RS):** Tr in 5th ch from hook, * ch 1, miss 1 ch, tr in next ch, * repeat to end, turn [45 (55, 65, 75) spaces.]
**Row 2 (WS):** Ch 4, * tr in next tr, ch 1, * repeat to end, tr in 3rd turning ch, turn.
**Row 3:** Ch 4, tr in next tr, ch 1, * tr in next tr, work 4lps in next ch sp, (tr in next tr, ch 1) repeat 15 times, repeat from * 1 (2, 3, 3) times, tr in next tr, work 4lps in next ch sp, (tr in next tr, ch 1) repeat 10 (4, 14, 8) times, tr in 3rd turning ch, turn.
**Row 4:** Ch 4, (tr in next tr, ch 1) repeat 8 (2, 12, 6) times, * tr in next tr, work 4lps in next ch sp, tr in next tr, ch 1, tr in next tr, work 4lps in next ch sp *, (tr in next tr, ch 1) repeat 13 times *, repeat from * to * 1 (2, 3, 3) times, tr in next tr, work 4lps in next ch sp, tr in next tr, ch 1, tr in next tr, work 4lps in next ch sp, tr in next tr, ch 1, tr in 3rd turning ch, turn.
**Row 5:** Work as row 3.
**Rows 6, 7 and 8:** Work as row 2.
**Row 9:** Ch 4, (tr in next tr, ch 1) repeat 9 times, * tr in next tr, work 4lps in next ch sp, (tr in next tr, ch 1) repeat 15 times, repeat from * 1 (1, 2, 2) times, tr in next tr, work 4lps in next ch sp, (tr in next tr, ch 1) repeat 2 (12, 6, 16) times, tr in 3rd turning ch, turn.
**Row 10:** Ch 4, (tr in next tr, ch 1) repeat 0 (10, 4, 14) times, * tr in next tr, work 4lps in next ch sp, tr in next tr, ch 1, tr in next tr, work 4lps in next ch sp ** (tr in next tr, ch 1) repeat 13 times *, repeat from * to * 1 (1, 2, 2) times, then repeat from * to ** once more, (tr in next tr, ch 1) repeat 9 times, dc in 3rd turning ch, turn.
**Row 11:** Work as row 9.
**Rows 12, 13 and 14:** Work as row 2.
Repeat rows 3-12. Piece measures 24cm (9½in) ending with a WS row.

**Row 25 (dec row):** Ch 3, tr in next tr, (ch 1, tr in next tr) repeat 42 (52, 62, 72) times, ch 1, tr in next tr, tr in 3rd turning ch, turn.
**Row 26:** Ch 4, miss next tr, * tr in next tr, ch 1, * repeat 42 times, miss

next tr, tr in turning ch, turn. 43 (53, 63, 73) spaces.

**Row 27:** Ch 4, (tr in next tr, ch 1) repeat 16 times, tr in next tr, work 4lps in next ch sp, * (tr in next tr, ch 1) repeat 15 times, tr in next tr, work 4lps in next ch sp *, repeat from * 0 (1, 1, 2) times, (tr in next tr, ch 1) repeat 9 (3, 13, 7) times, tr in 3rd turning ch, turn.

**Row 28:** Ch 4, (tr in next tr, ch 1) repeat 7 (1, 11, 5) times, * tr in next tr, work 4lps in next ch sp, tr in next tr, ch 1, tr in next tr, work 4lps in next ch sp, (tr in next tr, ch 1) repeat 13 times, * repeat from * to * 0 (1, 1, 2) times, tr in next tr, work 4lps in next ch sp, tr in next tr, ch 1, tr in next tr, work 4lps in next ch sp, (tr in next tr, ch 1) repeat 16 times, tr in 3rd turning ch, turn.

**Row 29:** Work as row 27.

**Row 30 (dec row):** Ch 3, tr in next tr, (ch 1, tr in next tr) repeat 40 (50, 60, 70) times, ch 1, tr in next tr, tr in 3rd turning ch, turn.

**Row 31:** Ch 4, miss next tr, (tr in next tr, ch 1) repeat 40 (50, 60, 70) times, miss next tr, tr in turning ch, turn. 41 (51, 61, 71) spaces.

### Double crochet band

**Row 1:** Ch 1, (dc in next ch sp, dc in next tr) repeat to end, end with dc in 3rd turning ch, turn. 82 (102, 122, 142) dc.

**Rows 2-8:** Ch 1, dc in each dc to end, turn.

**Row 9:** Ch 1, dc in each dc to end, end with 2 dc into turning ch, turn. 83 (103, 123, 143) dc.

### Crossed treble crochet pattern and armhole shaping

**Row 1:** Ch 3, ctc to end of row, end with tr in turning ch, turn. 41 (51, 61, 71) ctr.

**Row 2:** Ch 1, dc in each dc to end, turn.

**Rows 3-14:** Work last 2 rows a total of 7 times.

**Row 15:** Ch 1, sl st in next 6 (6, 8, 8) dc, ch 3, ctr 35 (45, 53, 63) times, tr in next dc, leaving last 6 sts unworked, turn. 35 (45, 53, 63) ctr.

**Row 16:** Ch 1, dc in next dc, dc3tog, dc to last 4 sts, dc3tog, dc in next dc, dc in turning ch.

**Row 17:** Work as row 1. 33 (43, 51, 61) ctr.

**Row 18:** Work as row 16.

**Rows 19-22:** Work last 2 rows a total of 3 times. 27 (37, 45, 55) ctr.

**Row 23:** Work as row 1.

**Row 24:** Work as row 2.

Work last 2 rows a total of 8 (8, 9, 10) times. 27 (37, 45, 55) ctr.

### Back right neck shaping

**Row 38 (38, 40, 42):** Ch 3, 6 (10, 13, 17) ctr, 1 tr in next tr, turn. Leave remaining sts unworked. 6 (10, 13, 17) ctr.

**Row 39 (39, 41, 43):** 1 dc in next dc, dc3tog, dc to end, turn.

### Back left neck shaping

**Row 38 (38, 40, 42):** Miss next 30 dc, rejoin yarn, ch 3, ctr to end of row, end with tr in turning ch, turn (6 ctr).

**Row 39 (39, 41, 43):** Ch 1, dc in each dc to the last 4 sts, dc3tog, dc in next dc, end with dc in turning ch, turn.

### FRONT
Work as for back completing row 24 of ctr patt and armhole shaping.

### Left neck shaping

**Row 25:** Ch 3, 10 (14, 17, 21) ctr, 1 tr in next tr, turn. Leave remaining sts unworked. 10 (14, 17, 21) ctr.

**Row 26:** Ch 1, dc in next dc, dc3tog, dc to end, turn.

**Row 27:** Ch 3, ctr to end of row, end with tr in turning ch, turn.

**Rows 28-35:** Work last 2 rows until 5 (9, 12, 16) ctr.

**Row 36:** Ch 1, dc in each dc to end, turn.

**Row 37:** Work as row 27.

Repeat last 2 rows until armhole measures same as back.

### Right neck shaping

**Row 25:** Miss next 12 (16, 20, 24) dc, rejoin yarn, ch 3, ctr to end of row, end with tr in turning ch, turn.

**Row 26:** Ch 1, dc in each tr to the last 4 sts, dc3tog, dc in next tr, end with dc in turning ch, turn.

**Row 27:** Ch 3, ctr to end of row, end with tr in turning ch, turn. 10 (14, 17, 21) ctr.

**Rows 28-35:** Work last 2 rows a total of until 5 (9, 12, 16) ctr.

**Row 36:** Ch 1, dc in each dc to end, turn.

**Row 37:** Work as row 27.

Repeat last 2 rows until armhole measures same as other side.

### SLEEVES
Ch 51 (51, 55, 59).

### Flower mesh pattern

**Row 1 (RS):** Tr in 5th ch from hook, * ch 1, miss 1 ch, tr in next ch, * repeat to end, turn. 23 (23, 25, 27) spaces.

**Row 2 (WS):** Ch 4, * tr in next tr, ch 1, * repeat to end, tr in 3rd turning ch, turn.

**Row 3:** Ch 4, (tr in next tr, ch 1) repeat 2 (2, 3, 4) times, tr in next tr, work 4lps in next ch sp, (tr in next tr, ch 1) repeat 15 times, tr in next tr, work 4lps in next ch sp, (tr in next tr, ch 1) repeat 3 (3, 4, 5) times, tr in 3rd turning ch, turn.

**Row 4:** Ch 4, (tr in next tr, ch 1) repeat 1 (1, 2, 3) times, tr in next tr, work 4lps in next ch sp, tr in next tr, ch 1, tr in next tr, work 4lps in next ch sp, (tr in next tr, ch 1) repeat 13 times, tr in next tr, work 4lps in next ch sp, tr in next tr, ch 1, tr in next tr, work 4lps in next ch sp, (tr in next tr, ch 1) repeat 2 (2, 3, 4) times, tr in 3rd turning ch, turn.

**Row 5:** Work as row 3.

**Rows 6, 7 and 8:** Work as row 2.

**Row 9:** Ch 4, (tr in next tr, ch 1) repeat 10 (10, 11, 12) times, tr in next tr, work 4lps in next ch sp, (tr in next tr, ch 1) repeat 11 (11, 12, 13) times, tr in 3rd turning ch, turn.

**Row 10:** Ch 4, (tr in next tr, ch 1) repeat 9 (9, 10, 11) times, tr in next tr, work 4lps in next ch sp, tr in next tr, ch 1, tr in next tr, work 4lps in next ch sp, (tr in next tr, ch 1) repeat 10 (10, 11, 12) times, tr in 3rd turning ch, turn.

**Row 11 (inc row):** Ch 4, (1 tr, ch 1, 1 tr) in next tr, (ch 1, tr in next tr) repeat 10 (10, 11, 12) times, work 4lps in next ch sp, (tr in next tr, ch 1) repeat 10 (10, 11, 12) times, (1 tr, ch 1, 1 tr) in next tr, ch 1, tr in 3rd turning ch, turn. 25 (25, 27, 29) spaces.

**Rows 12, 13 and 14:** Work as row 2.

**Row 15 (inc row):** Ch 4, (1 tr, ch 1, 1 tr) in next tr, (ch 1, tr in next tr) repeat 3 (3, 4, 5) times, work 4lps in next ch sp, (tr in next tr, ch 1) repeat 15 times, tr in next tr, work 4lps in next ch sp, (tr in next tr, ch 1) repeat 3 (3, 4, 5) times, (1 tr, ch 1, 1 tr), in next tr, ch 1, tr in 3rd turning ch, turn. 25 (25, 27, 29) spaces.

**Row 16:** Ch 4, (tr in next tr, ch 1) repeat 3 (3, 4, 5) times, tr in next tr, work 4lps in next ch sp, tr in next tr, ch 1, tr in next tr, work 4lps in next ch sp, (tr in next tr, ch 1) repeat 13 times, tr in next tr, work 4lps in next ch sp, tr in next tr, ch 1, tr in next tr, work 4lps in next ch sp, (tr in next tr, ch 1) repeat 4 (4, 5, 6) times, tr in 3rd turning ch, turn.

**Row 17:** Ch 4, (tr in next tr, ch 1) repeat 4 (4, 5, 6) times, work 4lps in next ch sp, (tr in next tr, ch 1) repeat 15 times, tr in next tr, work 4lps in next ch sp, (tr in next tr, ch 1) repeat 4 (4, 5, 6) times, tr in 3rd turning ch, turn.

**Rows 18 and 20:** Work as row 2.

**Row 19 (inc row):** Ch 4, (1 tr, ch 1, 1 tr), in next tr, (ch 1, tr in next tr) repeat 25 (25, 27, 29) times, (1 tr, ch 1, 1 tr), in next tr, ch 1, tr in 3rd turning ch, turn. 29 (29, 31, 33) spaces.

**Row 21:** Ch 4, (tr in next tr, ch 1) repeat 13 (13, 14, 15) times, tr in next tr, work 4lps in next ch sp, (tr in next tr, ch 1) repeat 14 (14, 15, 16) times, tr in 3rd turning ch, turn.

**Row 22:** Ch 4, (tr in next tr, ch 1) repeat 12 (12, 13, 14) times, tr in next tr, work 4lps in next ch sp, tr in next tr, ch 1, tr in next tr, work 4lps in next ch sp, (tr in next tr, ch 1) repeat 13 (13, 14, 15) times, tr in 3rd turning ch, turn.

**Row 23 (inc row):** Ch 4, (1 tr, ch 1, 1 tr) in next tr, (ch 1, tr in next tr) repeat 13 (13, 14, 15) times, work 4lps in next ch sp, (tr in next tr, ch 1) repeat 13 (13, 14, 15) times, (1 tr, ch 1, 1 tr) in next tr, ch 1, tr in 3rd turning ch, turn. 31 (31, 33, 35) spaces.

**Rows 24, 25 and 26:** Work as row 2.

**Row 27 (inc row):** Ch 4, (1 tr, ch 1, 1 tr) in next tr, (ch 1, tr in next tr)

repeat 6 (6, 7, 8) times, work 4lps in next ch sp, (tr in next tr, ch 1) repeat 15 times, tr in next tr, work 4lps in next ch sp, (tr in next tr, ch 1) repeat 6 (6, 7, 8) times, (1 tr, ch 1, 1 tr) in next tr, ch 1, tr in 3rd turning ch, turn. 33 (33, 35, 37) spaces.

**Row 28:** Ch 4, (tr in next tr, ch 1) repeat 6 (6, 7, 8) times, tr in next tr, work 4lps in next ch sp, tr in next tr, ch 1, tr in next tr, work 4lps in next ch sp, (tr in next tr, ch 1) repeat 13 times, tr in next tr, work 4lps in next ch sp, tr in next tr, ch 1, tr in next tr, work 4lps in next ch sp, (tr in next tr, ch 1) repeat 7 (7, 8, 9) times, tr in 3rd turning ch, turn.

**Row 29:** Ch 4, (tr in next tr, ch 1) repeat 7 times, work 4lps in next ch sp, (tr in next tr, ch 1) repeat 15 times, tr in next tr, work 4lps in next ch sp, (tr in next tr, ch 1) repeat 8 (8, 9, 10) times, tr in 3rd turning ch, turn.

**Rows 30 and 31:** Work as row 2. 33 (33, 35, 57) spaces.

## Double crochet band

**Row 1:** Ch 1, (dc in next ch sp, dc in next tr) repeat to end, end with dc in 3rd turning ch, turn. 66 (66, 70, 74) dc.

**Row 2-8:** Ch 1, dc in each dc to end, turn.

**Row 9:** Ch 1, dc in each dc to end, end with 2 dc into turning ch, turn. 67 (67, 71, 75) dc.

## Crossed treble crochet pattern

**Row 1:** Ch 3, ctr to end of row, end with tr in turning ch, turn. 33 (33, 35, 37) ctr.

**Row 2:** Ch 1, dc in each dc to end, turn.

Work rows 1 and 2 a total of 7 (7, 8, 9) times.

## Cap shaping

**Row 1:** Ch 1, sl st in next 6 (6, 8, 10) dc, ch 3, ctr 27 times, tr in next dc, leaving last 6 (6, 8, 10) sts unworked, turn. 27 ctr.

**Row 2:** Ch 1, dc in next dc, dc3tog, dc to last 4 sts, dc3tog, dc in next dc, dc in turning ch.

**Row 3:** Ch 3, ctr to end of row, end with tr in turning ch, turn. 25 ctr.

**Row 4:** Work as row 2.

**Work** last 2 rows a total of 3 times. 19 ctr.

## FINISHING

Block the crocheted pieces lightly (see page 137).
With yarn and tapestry needle, sew shoulder seams.
Position sleeves in armhole opening, sew in place.
Sew sleeve and side seams. Weave in all loose ends.

## Edgings

Dc 1 row around neck opening, lower edge of sleeve and lower edge of sweater.

This gorgeous lilac swing cardigan is oh-so-pretty, with its decorative yoke and unusual floral tie fastenings. Instead of using ribbon, the designer has torn up strips of floral Liberty fabric and woven these through the treble crochet rows, giving a contemporary twist and a unique feel to this lovely piece. This is a great way to reinvent favourite dresses or vintage silk scarves that have seen better days – don't worry if the fabric frays, it will add to the charm.

# 'Millie' Cardigan    Alicia Paulson

## MATERIALS

Twelve (fourteen, fifteen, sixteen) 50g balls Debbie Bliss Cashmerino
  Aran, shade 012 Dusky Pink
4mm crochet hook
4.25mm crochet hook
Three strips of fabric, each approximately 115cm (1¼yds) long and
  1.5cm (⅝in) wide
Tapestry needle
Stitch marker

## MEASUREMENTS

**To fit four sizes:** S (M, L, XL).
**Bust measurement:** 97 (102, 112, 122)cm/38 (40, 44, 48)in.
**Length:** 43 (43, 44, 44)cm/17 (17, 17½, 17½)in.
**Sleeve length:** 43 (43, 44, 44)cm/17 (17, 17½, 17½)in.

## NOTE

Instructions for larger sizes are given in parentheses. Where there is only one figure, it applies to all sizes.

## TENSION

16 sts and 19 rows = 10cm (4in) in body pattern stitch using a 4.25mm crochet hook.

## ABBREVIATIONS

See page 120.

## YOKE

Using smaller hook, ch 71.
**Row 1 (RS):** Tr in 4th ch from hook, tr in each ch across to end, turn (68 sts).
**Row 2:** Ch 3 (counts as first tr), (tr in next tr, 2 tr in next tr, tr in next tr) 22 times, tr in next tr, turn (90 sts).
**Row 3:** Ch 3, tr in each tr across to end, turn (90 sts).
**Row 4:** Ch 3, (1 tr in next tr, 2 tr in next tr, tr in next 2 tr) 22 times, tr in last tr, turn (112 sts).
**Row 5:** Repeat row 3 (112 sts).
**Row 6:** Ch 3, (tr in next 2 tr, 2 tr in next tr, tr in next 2 tr) 22 times, tr in next tr, turn (134 sts).
**Row 7:** Repeat row 3 (134 sts).
**Row 8:** Ch 3, (tr in next 3 tr, 2 tr in next tr, tr in next 2 tr) 22 times, tr in next tr, turn (156 sts).
**Row 9:** Repeat row 3 (156 sts).

**Divide yoke for sizes S and M**
**Row 10:** Ch 3, (tr in next 3 tr, 2 tr in next tr, tr in next 3 tr) 22 times (178 sts).
**Row 11:** Repeat row 3 (178 sts).

**Divide yoke for sizes L and XL**
**For left front:** Place marker at st 22 (22, 26, 26) from edge.
**For left sleeve:** Place marker at st 34 (34, 38, 38) from edge of left front (in other words, start counting from last st of left front, or at st 23 from edge).
**For back:** Place marker at st 44 (44, 52, 52) from edge of left sleeve.
**For right sleeve:** Place marker at st 34 (34, 38, 38) counted from edge of back piece.
**For right front:** You should have 22 (22, 26, 26) sts (including 1st ch-3, which counted as 1st dc).

## LEFT FRONT

**Row 1:** With larger hook, ch 1, miss first tr, 2 dc in next tr, (miss next tr, 2 dc in next tr) 10 (10, 12, 12) times more, dc in last st (inc made), turn [23 (23, 27, 27) sts].

**Row 2:** Ch 1, 2 dc in 1st dc (inc made), 2 dc in next dc, (miss next dc, 2 dc in next dc) 10 (10, 12, 12) times, turn [24 (24, 28, 28) sts].
Repeat rows 1-2 fourteen (16, 16, 20) times more [38 (40, 44, 48) sts].
Continue straight for 46 (46, 48, 48) rows more until left front measures 33 (34, 36, 37)cm/13 (13½, 14, 14½)in from bottom of yoke (not neckline).

## LEFT SLEEVE

**Row 1:** With larger hook, attach yarn with sl st in next st over from edge of left front. Ch 1, dc in same dc as ch-1, 2 dc in next dc (inc made), (miss next dc, 2 dc in next dc) 16 (16, 18, 18) times, dc again in last dc (inc made), turn [36 (36, 40, 40) sts].

**Row 2:** Ch 1, 2 dc in first dc, 2 dc in next dc, (miss next dc, 2 dc in next dc) 17 (17, 19, 19) times, 2 dc in last dc, turn [38 (38, 42, 42) sts].
Repeat rows 1-2 fourteen (16, 16, 20) times more [66 (70, 74, 82) sts].
Continue straight for 46 (46, 48, 48) rows more until sleeve measures 33 (34, 36, 37)cm/13 (13½, 14, 14½)in from bottom of yoke (not neckline).

## BACK

**Row 1:** With larger hook, attach yarn with sl st in next st over from edge of left sleeve. Ch 1, dc in same dc as ch-1, 2 dc in next dc (inc made), (miss next dc, 2 dc in next dc) 21 (21, 25, 25) times, dc again in last dc (inc made), turn [46 (46, 54, 54) sts].

**Row 2:** Ch 1, 2 dc in first dc, 2 dc in next dc, (miss next dc, 2 dc in next dc) 22 (22, 26, 26) times, 2 dc in last dc, turn [48 (48, 56, 56) sts].
Repeat rows 1-2 fourteen (16, 16, 20) times more [76 (80, 88, 96) sts].
Continue straight for 46 (46, 48, 48) rows more until back measures 33 (34, 36, 37)cm/13 (13½, 14, 14½)in from bottom of yoke (not neckline).

## RIGHT SLEEVE

**Row 1:** With larger hook, attach yarn with sl st in next st over from edge of back. Work as for left sleeve, reversing shaping.

## RIGHT FRONT

**Row 1:** With larger hook, attach yarn with sl st in next st over from edge of right sleeve. Work as for left front, reversing shaping.

## FINISHING

Sew sleeves to fronts and back. Sew up sides, and then underarms. With RS facing, join yarn at left side seam. Dc in bottom loop of each dc across back and right front. Make 3 dc in last stitch of right front to turn corner. Dc evenly up right front and yoke, and in each loop of trs around neck opening. Make 3 dc in last stitch of neck to turn corner down yoke. DC down edge of yoke and left front, making 3 dc around corner of left front, and continue across bottom of left front. Join with sl st into first dc. Fasten off.

Weave in all ends and block lightly (see page 137).
Weave fabric strips through trs around yoke where comfortable, and tie in a bow to close.

As well as making a fashion statement, this retro kerchief is a great way to keep the wind at bay or keep your head warm when it's chilly outside. The body of the headscarf is made in zigzag ric-rac stitch with a pretty picot edging. The ribbon woven through the eyelets can be in either a matching or contrasting colour.

# Ric-Rac Kerchief

## Juju Vail

### MATERIALS

Debbie Bliss Baby Cashmerino in the following quantities and shades:
   Two 50g balls shade 103 Peach (Yarn A)
   One ball shade 11 Brown (Yarn B)
3mm crochet hook
Tapestry needle
70cm (28in) mint coloured velvet ribbon, 1cm (½in) wide
Needle and thread to match ribbon colour

### MEASUREMENTS

**Length from edge of headband to tip of triangle:** 40cm (16in).
**Width across base of triangle:** 57cm (22in).
**Width including tie:** 82cm (32in).

### TENSION

Make a tension swatch of ric-rac stitch, as follows. Make a base chain of 21 plus two ch to turn. Follow instructions for ric-rac stitch for 14 rows, making every 4th row in an alternate colour. This should make a swatch of 10 x 10cm (4 x 4in).

### ABBREVIATIONS

See page 120.

## RIC-RAC STITCH

Work stitch over number of chains divisible by 3, plus two chains to turn.

**Row 1:** Into 4th chain from hook work (1 tr, 2 ch, 1 dc), * miss next 2 ch, (1 tr, 2 ch, 1 dc) into next ch, rep from * to end. Turn.

**Row 2:** 3 ch, (1 tr, 2 ch, 1 dc) into first 2-ch space, * (1 tr, 2 ch, 1 dc) into next 2-ch space, rep from * to end. Turn.

The last row is repeated throughout to form the pattern. Every 4th row is worked in an alternate colour.

## KERCHIEF RIBBON BAND

With Yarn A, make base row of 111 ch plus two to turn.

**Row 1:** Switch to Yarn B. Dc 1 row, starting with 3rd ch from hook.

**Row 2:** 2 ch, repeat row 1.

**Row 3 (eyelet row):** * 2 htr, 1 ch, miss next st *. Repeat 35 times, make 3 htr, turn.

**Rows 4 and 5:** Repeat row 2.

## RIC-RAC FABRIC AND DECREASES

**Row 1 (ric-rac stitch):** With Yarn A, work 1st row of ric-rac stitch into top loops of 110 sts from previous row (miss final loop).

For rows 1, 2 and 3 of the pattern use Yarn A, and for row 4 use Yarn B. Cut and rejoin the yarn for each colour change.

**Row 2:** Continue in ric-rac stitch over the 110 sts, making decreases (see instructions below) on rows 2 and 3 of Yarn A for the first 27 rows. Therefore, these decreases will appear on the following rows: 2, 3, 6, 7, 10, 11, 14, 15, 18, 19, 22, 23, 26 and 27.

After row 27, the decreases will occur every row for the next 5¾ repeats of the pattern, ending with 3 rows of Yarn A. This will make a total of 50 rows. Pull yarn through final loop.

**To make a decrease:** 3 ch, miss the first 2-ch space and work into the second 2-ch space. Continue to end of row as usual.

## TIE EXTENSION

**Row 1:** Using Yarn B, make 6 dc into the edge stitches of the ribbon band.

**Row 2:** 2 ch, 6 dc, turn.

Make 20 rows and then decrease 1 stitch on each side until 1 stitch remains (forming a point). Cut yarn and pull through stitch. Repeat for other end of tie.

## EDGE STITCH

Beginning with top left edge of ribbon band (where Yarn A leaves off edging Yarn B), work dc in Yarn A around the outside edge of Yarn B ribbon band.

Continue around band point, working 3 dcs into the top point of band to pivot.

Dc until you reach the ric-rac stitch and then work in picot-edge stitch as follows.

### Picot-edge stitch

**Row 1:** 3 dc into Yarn A edge loop, 3 dc into Yarn B edge loop. Repeat until you reach the tip (26 dc). Make 3 dc into loop at tip of scarf and then continue down other side as before. Stop at the end of the ric-rac fabric, turn.

**Row 2:** * 5 ch, sl st into 2nd ch from hook, 2 ch, dc into the 3rd dc loop from previous row. * Continue making picot edging all around ric-rac fabric of kerchief.

Cut yarn and pull through last stitch to fasten off.

Using Yarn A, go back to unfinished edge of Yarn B ribbon band and make sl sts around outer edge as for the first tie edge.

## FINISHING

Darn all yarn ends into the crochet fabric securely and trim. Thread ribbon through the holes in the band and secure with a few stitches, using sewing needle and thread, on the wrong side of both ends.

Sweet little crochet rosettes are fashioned into a short-sleeve waist-length shrug, named for favourite World War 2 pin-up girl Betty Grable. Made from delicious Blue Sky Alpacas sportweight yarn in soft nickel grey, the motifs can be worked one at a time and joined into the finished garment as you go, so seaming is kept to a minimum. Fasten with a pretty button or brooch.

# 'Betty' Shrug  Kristeen Griffin-Grimes

## MATERIALS
**Size S-M:** Seven 50g balls Blue Sky Alpacas Sportweight Baby Alpaca yarn, shade 524 Nickel
**Sizes L and XL:** Eight balls of yarn, as above
**Size S-M:** 3.75mm crochet hook
**Sizes L and XL:** 4.25mm crochet hook
Stitch marker

## MEASUREMENTS
**To fit three sizes:** S-M, L, XL.
**Back length:** 41 (44, 46)cm/16 (17½, 18)in measured from top to point of bottom motif.
**Sleeve length at underarm:** 16 (18, 20)cm/6½ (7, 8)in.
**Width at hem:** 99 (112, 120)cm/39 (44, 47½)in.
Garment is constructed so that front edges hang lower than back hem.

## NOTE
Instructions for larger sizes are given in parentheses. Where there is only one figure, it applies to all sizes.

## TENSION
**Motif size:** 14 x 14cm (5½ x 5½in) using a 3.75mm crochet hook.
15.5 x 15.5cm (6 x 6in) using a size 4.25mm hook.

## SPECIAL ABBREVIATIONS
**M + number:** Motif with number referring to the diagram (on page 39).
**tr2tog:** Work 1 tr leaving 2 loops remaining on hook, work 2nd tr into same st, until there are 3 loops remaining, then complete both sts as 1 st, by yrh and pulling yarn through all 3 loops on hook.
**tr3tog cluster (tr3tog cl):** Work 1 tr leaving 2 loops on hook, work 2nd tr into same st until 3 loops remain, work 3rd tr until 4 loops remain, then yrh, pull yarn through 2 loops, yrh, pull yarn through remaining 3 loops.
**tr4tog cluster (tr4tog cl):** Work 1 tr leaving 2 loops on hook, work 2nd tr into same st until 3 loops remain, work 3rd tr until 4 loops remain, work 4th tr until 5 loops remain then yrh, pull yarn through 2 loops (4 loops remain), yrh, pull yarn through remaining 4 loops.

## MOTIFS
### Motif 1
**Round 1:** Form circle to begin the motif as follows:
Holding short tail of yarn taut, wrap yarn around index finger twice. Keeping circle intact and continuing to hold short tail in place, insert crochet hook into opening in circle and draw through loop, ch 3 (counts as 1 tr). Place 15 more tr in the ring (16 total tr). Join the last tr with a sl st to 3rd ch of first ch-3. As you work, tighten up opening in circle until, after all sts are placed for first round, the circle is completely closed.
**Round 2:** Ch 4 (counts as 1 tr + ch-1), (1 tr, ch-1) in each of the next 15 tr in ring. Join with sl st to 4th ch in first ch-4.
**Round 3:** Ch 3, tr2tog into same space as ch-3 (counts as 1 cluster), then ch 2, (tr3tog, ch 2) into 15 remaining ch-1 spaces from round 2, ending last cluster with tr3tog, then tr into top of first tr2tog (16 cluster sts made).
**Round 4:** Ch 1, dc into top of 1st tr2tog from round 3 (same spot you placed joining tr at end of round 3). * Ch 5, dc into ch-2 space from round 3, repeat from * until last ch-2 space. Ch 2, then tr into dc at beginning of round.
**Round 5:** Ch 3, then (tr3tog, ch 3, tr4tog) into the space in last ch loop from round 4 (1st corner cluster made). * (Ch 5, dc into next ch-5 loop) 3 times, ch 5, place (tr4tog cl, ch 3, tr4tog cl) into the next ch-5 loop from round 4 (2nd corner cluster made). Continue around motif repeating from * making 3rd corner cluster and ending with ch 5 in 1st tr3tog at beginning of round. Fasten off yarn.

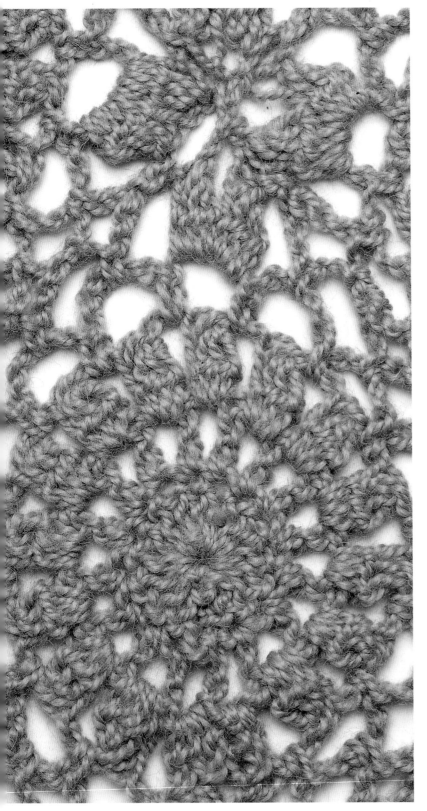

## Motif 2

After completing motif 1, work motif 2 to the end of round 4 and, referring to the chart on page 39, join them in this manner: learn to recognize where the corners of the motifs will fall to aid in joining motifs.

**Sizes S-M and L:** On M2 begin round 5, work up to 3rd tr4tog cluster group (3rd corner) and join to M1: ** make 1 tr4tog cl, ch 1, sl st into ch-3 space between the 2 tr4tog cl on M1, ch 1, complete 2nd tr4tog cl on M2 **, * ch 2, sl st into ch-5 space on M1, ch 2, sl st into ch-5 space on M2, repeating from * until you reach the next corner. Repeat from ** to **, then ch 5 and complete remaining side as directed in round 5.

**Size XL:** On M2 begin round 5, work up to 3rd tr4tog cluster group (3rd corner) and join to M1: ** make 1 tr4tog cl, ch 2, sl st into ch-3 space between the 2 tr4tog cl on M1, ch 2, complete 2nd tr4tog cl on M2 **, * ch 3, sl st into ch-5 space on M1, ch 3, slip st into ch-5 space on M2, repeating from * until you reach the next corner. Repeat from ** to **, then ch 5 and complete remaining side as directed in round 5.

Join M3 to M1 in the same manner.

Join M4 to M1/2/3: This is the first of the motifs joined to the others on only 2 sides leaving a rounded edge (these motifs are denoted by a * on the chart).

Begin round 5 as directed above for M1, making only 1st cluster in M4, then ch 1, sl st into the ch-3 space between corner clusters on M2, continue to join sides of M4 and M2 as directed above until the next corner is reached, continuing in established pattern. Remember to sl st all the corner clusters together at the point where all motifs meet (into the ch-3 between the dc4tog cl), then continue in established joining pattern up the other side joining M4 to M3. End with ch 5 after 3rd corner is joined and sl st to ch-5 of round 4 on M4.

You will have now completed the first module of 4 motifs; the intersection where the 4 corners meet is the centre back line of garment. Continue to construct and join motifs in the order given, remembering to join the starred motifs to leave a rounded edge as directed above in joining M4. The starred motifs along the neckline will have the rounded edges at the top and the lower ones will have the rounded edges at the bottom.

Once you have completed joining the motifs to M20, construct 2 half motifs (M21 and M22) to complete the right and left fronts. These are made by working back and forth instead of in rounds.

## Motif 21

**Row 1:** Start motif as normal, placing only 10 tr in yarn ring. Turn.
**Row 2:** Work in established pattern, placing only 9 (tr, ch-1), ending with 1 tr in last tr from 1st round. Turn.

Shrug body

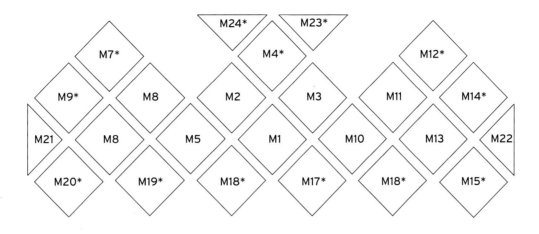

Sleeve front

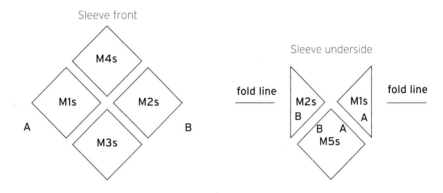

**Row 3:** Work in pattern, placing only 9 (tr3tog cluster, ch-2) end with 1 tr3tog cluster in tr from previous round. Turn.

**Row 4:** Ch 5, dc in next ch-2 space from previous round, repeat to end placing last dc in top of last tr3tog cluster from round 3. Leave yarn attached and attach to right and left fronts as follows.

Join M21 to M9 and M20.

**Sizes S–M and L:** Ch 5, sl st to ch-3 between 2 tr4tog clusters at left point of M20, ch 1, place 1 tr4tog cluster in 1st ch-5 loop on M21, ch 2, (sl st into next ch-5 loop on M20; ch 2, sl st into the next ch-5 loop on M21), repeat this twice more, ch 2, sl st into the last 5-ch loop before 4-tr cluster corner on M20, ch 2, place 1 tr4tog cluster in next ch-5 loop on M21, ch 1, sl st into point where M20, M8 and M9 join (this will be the ch-3 between tr4tog clusters in each of the corners of these motifs) ch 1, place the 2nd dc4tog cluster into the same ch-5 loop on M21 (2 clusters placed in same loop), then (ch 2, sl st into next ch-5 loop on M9, ch 2, sl st into next ch-5 loop on M21), repeat this twice more. Ch 2, sl st into last ch-5 loop before corner cluster on M9, ch 2,

place 1 tr4tog cluster in last ch-5 loop on M21, ch 1, sl st into ch-3 between 2 tr4tog clusters on M9, ch 5, sl sl st to last 5-ch loop from round 4 on M21. Fasten off.

**Size XL:** Ch 5, sl st to ch-3 between 2 tr4tog clusters at left point of M20, ch 2, place 1 tr4tog cluster in 1st ch-5 loop on M21, ch 3, (sl st into next ch-5 loop on M20; ch 3, sl st into the next ch-5 loop on M21), repeat this twice more, ch 3, sl st into the last 5-ch loop before 4-tr cluster corner on M20, ch 3, place 1 tr4tog cluster in next ch-5 loop on M21, ch 2, sl st into point where M20, M8 and M9 join (this will be the ch-3 between tr4tog clusters in each of the corners of these motifs, ch 2, place the 2nd dc4tog cluster into the same ch-5 loop on M21 (2 clusters placed in same loop), then (ch 3, sl st into next ch-5 loop on M9, ch 3, sl st into next ch-5 loop on M21), repeat this twice more. Ch 2, sl st into last ch-5 loop before corner cluster on M9, ch 3, place 1 tr4tog cluster in last ch-5 loop on M21, ch 2, sl st into ch-3 between 2 tr4tog clusters on M9, ch 5, sl st to last 5-ch loop from round 4 on M21. Fasten off yarn.

Join M22 in the same manner, starting by joining to M14 first, then to M15.

Complete the neckline to prepare for joining sleeves.
Before joining the sleeves and completing top edging, mark the following motifs:

**1.** The point where the right corner of M7 meets the top corner of M9 - for button placement (optional).
**2.** The point opposite that where the corner of M12 joins M14 - for button loop (optional).
**3.** Two places on M4: the 2nd ch-5 loop above both the left and right corner - for joining gusset M23 and M24.
**4.** The same point as in 3 above, on right side of M7 and left side of M12 - for aiding in sleeve placement.

## GUSSETS

Make 2 small gussets (M23 and M24) as follows:
Make and join M24 to M4.

**Row 1:** Begin motif in pattern, placing only 6 tr in yarn ring, not tightening up ring entirely for use in row 5. Turn.
**Row 2:** Ch 4 (counts as 1 tr + ch-1), place 4 more (1 tr, ch-1) in next 4 tr from round 1; tr in last tr. Turn.
**Row 3:** Repeat round 3 of pattern, placing 5 clusters (1 cluster + ch-2) in each of the ch-1 spaces from round 2. Turn.
**Row 4:** * Ch 5, dc into top ch-2 space from row 3, repeat from * to end, ending by sl st last ch-5 to last tr3tog cluster.
**Row 5:** Work around the left side, across the bottom point and up the right side of the gusset.
**Sizes S-M and L:** Ch 5, attach with sl st to dc from row 2; ch 5, ** place 1 tr3tog cluster in yarn ring, ch 1, sl st into corner cluster where M2 and M4 join, ch 1, place 1 tr3tog cluster in yarn ring, tighten up ring **. Continue joining M24 to M4. Ch 2, sl st to next ch-5 on M4, ch 2, sl st to tr from row 2 of M24; ch 2, sl st to next ch-5 on M4 (marked), ch 2, sl st to 1st ch-3 in row 3 of M24. Fasten off yarn.
**Size XL:** Ch 5, attach with sl st to dc from row 2; ch 5, ** place 1 tr3tog cluster in yarn ring, ch 2, sl st into corner cluster where M2 and M4 join, ch 2, place 1 tr3tog cluster in yarn ring, tighten up ring **. Continue joining M24 to M4. Ch 3, sl st to next ch-5 on M4, ch3, sl st to tr from row 2 of M24; ch 3, sl st to next ch-5 on M4 (marked), ch 3, sl st to 1st ch-3 in row 3 of M24. Fasten off yarn.

Make and join M24 to M4.
**Rows 1-4:** Complete M23 as rows 1-4 of M24.
**Row 5:** Work around the left side joining M23 to M4, across the bottom point, joining to M3 at its top point, then working up the right side preparing the edge for joining to the sleeve.

**Sizes S-M and L:** Ch 2, sl st to marked ch-5 (2nd ch-5 above corner tr4tog cluster on M4), ch 2, sl st to tr from row 2 of M23; ch 2, sl st into next ch-5 on M4, then ch-2 and repeat from ** to ** on row 5 above. Now working without joining to any motifs, ch 5, sl st into tr from row 2 on M23, ch 5, sl st to the 1st ch-3 in row 3 of M23. Keep yarn attached for use later (secure by safety pinning st closed).
**Size XL:** Ch 3, sl st to marked ch-5 (2nd ch-5 above corner tr4tog cluster on M4), ch 3, sl st to tr from row 2 of M23; ch 3, sl st into next ch-5 on M4, then ch-3 and repeat from ** to ** on row 5 above. Now working without joining to any motifs, ch 5, sl st into tr from row 2 on M23, ch 5, sl st to the 1st ch-3 in row 3 of M23. Keep yarn attached for use later (secure by safety pinning st closed).

## SLEEVES

**Right sleeve:** Complete M1s as M1 of garment body. Complete M2s as M1s, working row 5 and joining M1s and M2s at one corner, completing an entire row 5 around M2s. M3 and M4 will now be inserted into the two spaces to form the main sleeve: working in the same manner as M4 of body, join M3s and then M4s, making sure to leave two sides of each unworked to form the top and hem of sleeve (leave yarn attached). Complete M5s to row 4 of pattern, then, using row 5, join right edge to M1s (marked as A on chart), work into corners of M1s and M2s with tr4tog clusters as pattern, continue to finish joining to M2s (marked as B on chart), working in row 5 as written, making sure to leave two sides unworked for rounded lower edge of sleeve.

**Left sleeve:** Complete in same way as right sleeve.
Fasten off yarn.

Once sleeves are completed, on M5s mark the 2nd ch-5 above where round 5 begins and ends on each.

### Insert sleeves

For ease in placing sleeve, temporarily safety-pin corners of junction of M3, M10 and M11 on garment body to junction of M2s, M1s, and M4s on sleeve.

### Join right sleeve

**Sizes S-M and L:** Picking up yarn held back when joining M23 to garment, and working from the underside, ch 5, sl st to marked ch-5 on M5s, ch 2, sl st to last ch-5 from row 5 of M23, ch 2, sl st to next ch-5 in M23, ch 2, sl st into centre of dc4tog cluster where M5s and M1s join, ch 2, sl st into spot where M3, M4 and M23 join, ch 2, sl st into next ch-5 in M1s.
**Size XL:** Picking up yarn held back when joining M23 to garment, and working from the underside, ch 5, sl st to marked ch-5 on M5s,

ch 3, sl st to last ch-5 from row 5 of M23, ch 3, sl st to next ch-5 in M23, ch 3, sl st into centre of dc4tog cluster where M5s and M1s join, ch 3, sl st into spot where M3, M4 and M23 join, ch 3, sl st into next ch-5 in M1s.

Continue in this manner across underarm, working into the point where M1s, M2s and M4s (and M1, M3 and M11 join) as if it were a ch-5. Continue around, joining sleeve to body working up the side of M2s, treating the join of M2s and M5s, and M11 and M12, as a point to sl st into. Finish with established pattern at marked spot on M12. Leave yarn attached – complete top edge from this point after left sleeve is inserted.

### Join left sleeve
Attach yarn to spot marked on left top of M5s, ch 2, sl st to spot marked on M7, then continue in manner described for right sleeve to join sleeve to body, working around underarm, ending by joining M5s to M23, completing join at spot marked on right side of M5s. Fasten off yarn.

### Complete top edge
Taking up yarn held from joining right sleeve, mark that spot (this denotes beginning and end of top edge section).
Ch 5, sl st in the top of next ch-5 loop working from right to left across top edge and sleeve tops until marker on left edge of M7, * sl st in that loop, ch 2, tr into next ch. * Turn, ch 5, sl st into next ch-5 loop, working back across entire top edge over beginning point (move marker to current row), to right front edge marker on M12, repeat from * to *. Work back to beginning point (2 rows completed). Try on garment to determine how many more edging rows are needed. Garment as shown has 6 rows. If more rows are needed, work the next 2 rows (or more) with ch-4 instead of ch-5, ending with last 2 rows using ch-3. Work to beginning marker, fasten off yarn and weave in all ends.

### FINISHING
### Button and button loop
If desired, sew a vintage button on the left side at spot marked. On right side, attach yarn securely, make a ch with enough sts to slide securely over button; work back over ch with dc sts, fasten and secure yarn.

Block the garment lightly (see page 137).

This gorgeous hat and scarf set, made in rich berry-coloured cashmere worked in a textured bobble stitch with contrasting edging, is the ultimate in luxury. The super-soft yarn feels wonderful against the skin and will keep you feeling cosy and looking chic on the coldest of winter days.

# 'Lula' Scarf and Cloche Hat

## Juju Vail

### MATERIALS

**For scarf:** Three 55g balls Jade Sapphire 8-ply (Aran weight) Cashmere, shade 024 Plum Rose (Yarn A)

One 55g ball Jade Sapphire 6-ply (DK) Cashmere, shade 023 Pebble Beach (Yarn B)

**For cloche hat:** Three 55g balls Jade Sapphire 8-ply (Aran weight) Cashmere, shade 024 Plum Rose

4.5mm and 3mm crochet hooks

Tapestry needle

### MEASUREMENTS

**Scarf length:** 154cm (60½in); bobble end sections (x 2) 38cm (15in); middle sections (x 2) 30cm (12in) in Yarn A and 9cm (3½in) in Yarn B.

**Scarf width:** 16cm (6½in).

**Hat diameter at widest part of brim:** 32cm (12½in).

### TENSION

10 x 10cm (4 x 4in) = 8 rows x 5 cl using 4.5mm hook.

### ABBREVIATIONS

See page 120.

### SPECIAL ABBREVIATIONS

**cl – cluster:** 1 htr, 1 tr, 1 htr all in the same space.

**mb – make bobble:** Place yarn round hook, insert hook into ch, loop or space, yarn over hook and draw through a loop (3 loops on hook), yarn over hook and draw through 2 loops. Repeat this 5 times (6 loops on hook), yarn over hook and draw through all 6 loops.

### SCARF

#### Bobble ends

Using Yarn A and 4.5mm hook, 8 ch, turn. Dc in each st to end. Turn.

**Row 1:** 1 ch, mb, 2 dc, mb, 2 dc, mb. Turn

**Row 2:** 1 ch, 7 dc, 3 dc in last st on row. Turn.

**Row 3:** 1 ch, mb, 2 dc, mb, 2 dc, mb, 2 dc, mb. Turn.

**Row 4:** 1 ch, 3 dc in first st, 10 dc. Turn.

**Row 5:** 1 ch, * mb, 2 dc * 5 times. Turn.

**Row 6:** 1 ch, 13 dc, 3 dc in last st. Turn.

**Row 7:** 1 ch, * mb, 2 dc * 6 times. Turn.

**Row 8:** 1 ch, 3 dc in first st, 16 dc. Turn.

**Row 9:** 1 ch, * mb, 2 dc * 7 times. Turn.

**Row 10:** 1 ch, 19 dc, 3 dc in last st. Turn.

**Row 11:** 1 ch, * mb, 2 dc * 8 times. Turn.

**Row 12:** 1 ch, 21 dc. Turn.

**Row 13:** 1 ch, * 2 dc, mb * 8 times. Turn.

**Even rows 14, 16, 18, 20, 22, 24, 26 and 28:** Repeat row 12.

**Rows 15, 19, 23 and 27:** Repeat row 11.

**Rows 17, 21 and 25:** Repeat row 13.

#### Neck middle

Change to Yarn B.

**Row 1:** 2 ch, htr in next loop, * miss 2 loops, 1 cl in 3rd loop *, repeat 5 more times. Miss 1 loop, 2 htr in last loop. Turn.

**Row 2:** 2 ch, 1 cl in each of the next 7 spaces, 2 htr into last loop of row. Turn.

**Rows 3–8:** Repeat last row, ending each row with a half cluster (2 htr) into the last space.

Change yarn back to Yarn A and repeat row 2 twenty-nine times. Cut yarn and pull through loop to fasten off.

Repeat instructions from the beginning to make the other side of the scarf. Darn in ends and trim. Graft scarf middle backs together so that bobbles are both on the same side (see page 137).

### Contrasting trim

Using 3mm hook, begin crochet trim in Yarn B at the end of a bobble section (where Yarn B clusters begin).

Work 3 dc into the loop at the end of every other row. When you come to the beginning of the other side bobbles, cut yarn and pull through last stitch. Darn in end. Repeat for the other edge of scarf.

### CLOCHE HAT

The hat is worked in a circle so it is not turned between rows, but continues round. Using 4.5mm hook, ch 3, and join with sl st to form ring.

**Round 1:** 2 ch, 1 tr, 1 htr into centre of ring, work 3 cl into ring, join with sl st to beginning 3rd chain (12 sts into centre of ring).

**Round 2:** 2 ch, 1 tr, 1 htr into the same space as 2-ch, * miss 3 loops from previous row and work 1 cl between next stitches * (clusters are worked between groups of clusters, every 3 sts). Repeat from * twice, miss 3 sts and work final cl in same space as first cl, join with sl st to beginning 2-ch (24 sts or 8 cl).

**Round 3:** 2 ch, 1 tr, 1 htr into same space as 2-ch. * 2 cl between next pair of clusters, 1 cl between next pair of cl *. Repeat 2 more times, 1 cl in last space. Sl st to beginning 2-ch (36 sts or 12 cl).

**Round 4:** 2 ch, 1 tr, 1 htr into same space as 2-ch. * 1 cl between next cl, 1 cl between pair of cl, 2 cl between next cl *. Repeat from * twice. 1 cl between cl, 1 cl between cl, 1 cl in last space, sl st to beginning 2-ch (48 sts, or 16 cl).

**Round 5:** 2 ch, 1 tr, 1 htr into same space as 2-ch. * 2 cl between next cl, 1 cl in each of next 3 spaces between cl *. Repeat from * twice. 2 cl in next space between cl, 1 cl between each of next 2 cl. Sl st to beginning 2 ch (60 sts or 20 cl).

**Rounds 6-22:** 2 ch, 1 tr, 1 htr into same space as 2 ch. 1 cl between each pair of cl in previous row. Sl st to beginning 2-ch.

### Brim

Change to 3mm hook.

**Round 1:** 1 ch, 2 dc into the top of the stitch from previous row. Join ends with sl st to beginning ch.

**Rounds 2-4:** 1 ch, 1 dc into the top of the stitch from previous row. Join ends with sl st to beginning ch.

### TO FINISH

Darn yarn ends into hat and trim.

Using steam and very gentle pressure, block hat and brim into desired shape (see page 137).

These simple beads can be made in many types of yarn to create different textures and use up odd balls from your stash. They are filled with toy stuffing, so are very light to wear. You can play with the pattern by mixing different combinations of yarns and sizes of beads, as well as varying the spacing between them to create a fun and original accessory.

# 'Marianne' Bead Necklace    Claire Montgomerie

## MATERIALS
One 50g ball Blue Sky Alpacas Alpaca Silk in each of the following
    shades: 139 Peacock, 137 Sapphire, 136 Champagne
2.5mm crochet hook
Toy stuffing

## MEASUREMENTS
**Large beads:** Approximately 4cm (1¾in) diameter.
**Small beads:** Approximately 2.5cm (1in) diameter.
**Length of necklace:** Approximately 40cm (16in).

## TENSION
Tension not essential, but try to crochet tightly so that the toy stuffing cannot appear through the holes.

## ABBREVIATIONS
See page 120.

## NOTE
Use whatever type of yarn and hook you would like to create different beads.

## LARGE BEAD
Ch 2, 6 dc in 2nd ch from hook, join round with sl st to first dc.
**Round 1:** 2 dc in each dc around (12 sts). Sl st to join.
**Round 2:** (1 dc in next dc, 2 dc in next dc) around (18 sts). Sl st to join.
**Round 3:** Work 1 round straight in dc. Sl st to join.
**Round 4:** (1 dc into each of next 2 dc, 2 dc in next dc) around (24 sts). Sl st to join.
**Rounds 5-8:** Work 4 rows straight in dc. Sl st to join on each row.
Begin stuffing from now, as you start to close sphere, to hold shape.
**Round 9:** (Decrease by working 2dctog, 2 dc) around (18 sts). Sl st to join.
**Round 10:** Work 1 row straight in dc. Sl st to join.

**Round 11:** (Decrease as round 9, 1 dc) around (12 sts). Sl st to join.
**Rounds 12 and 13:** 2dctog around for next row and until you are left with 3 sts.
Fasten off yarn and weave closed.

Make 1 bead of each colour for necklace shown, or as many as you wish for necklace of your own design.

## SMALL BEAD
Ch 2, 6 dc in 2nd ch from hook, join round with sl st to first dc.
**Round 1:** 2 dc in each dc around (12 sts). Sl st to join.
**Round 2:** (1 dc in next dc, 2 dc in next dc) around (18 sts). Sl st to join.
**Rounds 3-6:** Work 4 rounds straight in dc. Sl st to join at end of each row.
Begin stuffing from now, as you start to close sphere, to hold shape.
**Round 7:** (Decrease by working 2dctog, 1 dc) around (12 sts). Sl st to join.
**Rounds 8-9:** 2dctog around for next row and until you are left with 3 sts.
Fasten off yarn and weave closed.

Make 3 or 4 beads in each colour for necklace shown, or as many as you wish for a necklace of your own design.

## CHAIN
Using 2.5mm hook, chain a length of approximately 80cm (32in), or until desired length of necklace is achieved. Thread all beads onto chain randomly. Join chain with sl st to first ch. Fasten off.

The perfect accessory for all hippie chicks, this wide spike-stitch hairband, with an extra-long tie worked in bobble stitch, looks great with short or long hair. Wear it with everything from flowing smock dresses to neat mini shifts, from skimpy shorts to slouchy jeans.

# 'Sienna' Headband    Bee Clinch

## MATERIALS

One 50g ball Blue Sky Alpacas Melange in each of the following
    shades: 800 Cornflower (Yarn A), 809 Toasted Almond (Yarn B),
    802 Pesto (Yarn C), 806 Salsa (Yarn D)
3.5mm crochet hook
Two vintage buttons, approximately 2-3cm (¾-1¼in) diameter
Tapestry needle

## MEASUREMENTS

**Length:** Main band 58cm (23in); ties 56cm (22in) each.
**Width, including edging:** 12cm (4¾in).

## TENSION

10 stitches over 6cm (2½in).

## ABBREVIATIONS

See page 120.

## SPECIAL ABBREVIATIONS

**sc2 - spiked crochet:** Be sure to insert hook into centre of the spikes 2 rows below the row you are working, yrh, draw through and up to height of row being worked, yrh, draw through both loops on hook. (See also page 129.)
**ps - puff stitch:** To make a puff stitch of 4 half treble stitches - yrh, insert the hook into the stitch, yrh again and draw a loop through (3 loops on the hook). Repeat this step 3 times more, inserting the hook into the same stitch each time (9 loops on hook), yrh, and draw through all loops on hook. (See page 123.)

## NOTES

The sequencing of colours is purely optional, but three different colours must be used for the main piece.

## HEADBAND

Measure head from base of right ear to base of left ear. For a scarf to fit size 45cm (18in), with Yarn A, ch 72. Adjust size according to yarn tension, but note that the spiked stitch pattern must be worked over a multiple of 10 + 2 sts.
**Row 1 (RS):** 1 dc into 2nd ch from hook, dc to end, ch 1, turn.
**Row 2:** With Yarn B, 1 dc into 1st st, dc to end, ch 1, turn.
**Row 3:** 1 dc into 1st st * 1 sc2 over each of next 5 sts, 1 dc in next 5 sts; repeat from * ending 1 dc into last dc, ch 1, turn.
**Rows 4-9:** Repeat the last 2 rows with Yarn C, followed with 2 rows in Yarn A, then 2 rows in Yarn B.
**Row 10:** With Yarn C, as 1st row.
**Row 11:** 1 dc in 1st st, * 1 dc in next 5 sts, 1 sc2 in next 5 sts; repeat from * ending 1 dc in last st, ch 1, turn.
**Rows 12-17:** Repeat the last 2 rows with Yarns A, Yarn B, then Yarn C. Repeat entire 17 rows once more. Fasten off.

## FINISHING

To mitre the ends of the headband, fold the corners at each end towards centre of headband to create a triangle at each end. Using yarn and a tapestry needle, sew the mitred ends in place securely.
**To picot the edge:** With Yarn D, beginning at straight edge, dc into 1st dc space on headband, * ch 3, sl st into 1 ch (picot made), dc into next dc on headband; repeat from * along straight edge to start of mitring. Continue with picots around mitred edge with at least 4 picots to each side of mitre. Repeat along other edge and mitre. Fasten off.
**Puff-stitch ties:** With Yarn D ch 4.
**Row 1:** 1 dc into 2nd ch, dc to end, 1 ch, turn.
**Row 2:** 1 dc in 1st st, ps in next st, 1 dc, ch 1, turn.
Repeat these 2 rows until tie measures approximately 45cm (18in), finishing with row 1. Fasten off.
Make another tie to match the first.
Press headband and ties lightly (see page 137).
Sew ties to wrong side of mitred corners of headband and sew the buttons on right side of mitred corners.

# Nostalgic Home

Wrap this colourful blanket around you for instant comfort and warmth, or throw it over your bed for a homespun look. The cheerful chevron stripes will lift your spirits and conjure up dreams of romantic snowy cabins in the woods, or cuddling up with a mug of hot chocolate after ice-skating.

# Chevron Blanket    Bee Clinch

## MATERIALS

Six 50g balls Rowan Cashsoft DK in each of the following shades:
  509 Lime (Yarn A), 501 Sweet (Yarn B), 517 Donkey (Yarn C),
  502 Bella Donna (Yarn D)
4mm crochet hook
Tapestry needle

## MEASUREMENTS

Approximately 120 x 180cm (48 x 72in). Blanket size can be adjusted easily as required using multiples of 12 sts + 3. To make a double size blanket, you will need twice as much yarn and should cast on twice the number of stitches.

## TENSION

18 stitches x 8 rows over 10cm (4in).

## ABBREVIATIONS

See page 120.

## SPECIAL ABBREVIATIONS

**tr2tog - ridged chevron in treble crochet:** To work 2 treble crochet together, wrap yarn round hook and insert in the next stitch, draw through the loop (3 loops on hook), wrap yarn round hook, draw through first 2 loops on hook (2 loops left on hook). Repeat the step on next stitch (3 loops left on hook). Wrap yarn round hook and draw through all 3 loops to complete group. Working under one loop, insert the hook into the back loop leaving the other loop as a bar to form a ridge across the row.

## BLANKET

Using Yarn A ch 216 + 3. Turn.
**Row 1:** 1 tr in 4th ch from hook, * 1 tr in next 3 ch (over next 2 sts work tr2tog) twice, 1 tr into each of next 3 sts, (2 tr into next st) twice; repeat from * ending last repeat with 2 tr into last ch, turn.

**Row 2:** 3 ch (counts as 1 tr), 1 tr into 1st st, always inserting hook into back loop only of each stitch, * 1 tr into each of next 3 sts, (over next 2 sts work tr2tog) twice, 1 tr into each of next 3 sts, (2 tr into next st) twice; repeat from * ending last repeat with 2 tr once only into top of tch, turn. Using Yarn B repeat row 2 twice.
Repeat row 2 twice in Yarn C and then in Yarn D. This sets the sequence to be repeated in all four colours until throw measures finished length.

## FINISHING

With tapestry needle sew all loose yarn ends into blanket.
Press lightly following yarn band instructions (see page 137).

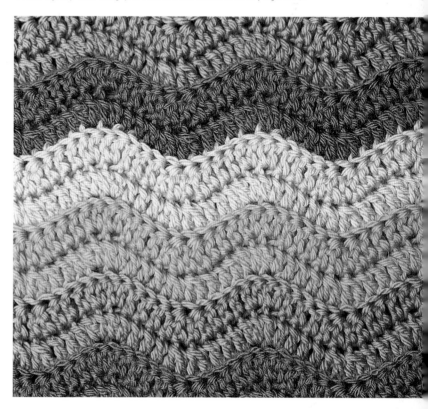

This gloriously vintage tablecloth conjures up the more relaxed pace of days gone by, when afternoon tea, complete with dainty china tea set and home-baked cakes, was a daily ritual for all the family. Perfect for special occasions, or to leave out all the time, this pretty tablecloth, made up of colourful picot squares, adds character to any table. You could also make a narrower version and use it as a runner.

# Picot Star Tablecloth

## Emma Seddon

### MATERIALS

Jaeger Siena 4-Ply Cotton in the following shades and quantities:
   Three 50g balls shade 412 Sapling (Yarn A)
   Three balls shade 432 Clover (Yarn B)
   Three balls shade 431 Sage (Yarn C)
   Three balls shade 433 Teak (Yarn D)
   Three balls shade 417 Blush (Yarn E)
   Four balls shade 430 Ocean (Yarn F)
3mm crochet hook
Tapestry needle

### MEASUREMENTS

Approximately 98 x 124cm (38½ x 49in).

### TENSION

One square should measure 12 x 12cm (5 x 5in).

### ABBREVIATIONS

See page 120.

### SPECIAL ABBREVIATIONS

MP - make picot: 3 ch, sl st into same sp.

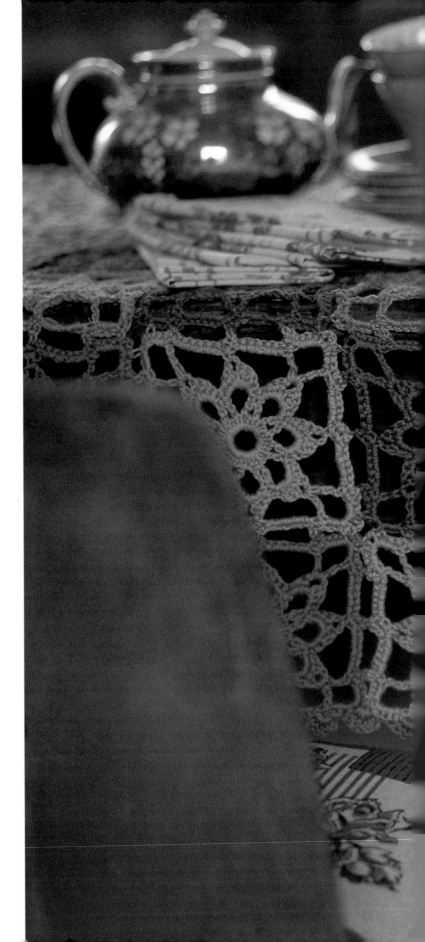

## PICOT SQUARE PATTERN

Make 14 in A
Make 14 in B
Make 13 in C
Make 12 in D
Make 13 in E
Make 14 in F
Total of 80 squares.

Ch 8, sl st to join into circle, 1 ch (see open ring method on page 126).

**Round 1:** 32 dc into ring, join with sl st.

**Round 2:** 8 ch (1 tr in next dc, miss 2 dc, 1 tr in next dc, 5 ch) 7 times, 1 tr in next dc, join with sl st to 3rd of 8 ch.

**Round 3:** Sl st into 5-ch space, (1 dc, 1 htr, 2 tr, 3 ch, 2 tr, 1 htr, 2 dc into same 5-ch space), * (1 dc, 1 htr, 2 tr, 3 ch, 2 tr, 1 htr, 2 dc into next 5-ch space), rep from * 7 more times, join with a sl st to 1st dc.

**Round 4:** Sl st along chains, up to the next 3-ch loop, 1 dc in same space, * 6 ch, (1 dtr, 5 ch, 1 dtr) in next 3-ch loop, 6 ch, 1 dc in next 3-ch loop, rep from * 3 more times, 6 ch, finish last repeat with a sl st into 1st dc.

**Round 5:** 1 dc into 1st dc made, * MP, 6 dc into 6-ch space, dc into dtr, MP, (4 dc, MP, 3 dc into 5-ch sp), 1 dc into dtr, MP, 6 dc into 6-ch sp, 1 dc into next dc, rep from * 3 more times, end last repeat with sl st into 1st dc.

## FINISHING

Block squares (see page 137).

With WS facing, lay squares out according to chart, above right. Using a tapestry needle and yarn of your choice sew the squares together by overcasting picots and corners together, carrying yarn through back of crochet between picots.

| B | C | D | E | F | A | B | C |
|---|---|---|---|---|---|---|---|
| A | B | C | D | E | F | A | B |
| F | A | B | C | D | E | F | A |
| E | F | A | B | C | D | E | F |
| D | E | F | A | B | C | D | E |
| C | D | E | F | A | B | C | D |
| B | C | D | E | F | A | B | C |
| A | B | C | D | E | F | A | B |
| F | A | B | C | D | E | F | A |
| E | F | A | B | C | D | E | F |

### Edging

With RS facing and using Yarn F, join into any central picot on a square - not on a corner, as it will be difficult to get a neat corner join.

3 ch, 4 tr in same space, miss 2 dc, sl st into next 2 dc, miss 2 dc, 5 tr into picot space, miss 2 dc, sl st into next 2 dc, 5 tr into join between squares, miss 2 dc, * sl st into next 2 dc, (5 tr into picot space, miss 2 dc, sl st into next 3 dc) twice, 5 tr into picot space, miss 2 dc. Repeat from * across each square and along each edge.

**Corners:** Work 5 tr into corner picot space as per pattern.

Finish off by slip stitching into the first 3 ch made and joining back to the main fabric of the cloth.

This funky cushion lends a laid-back modern-retro vibe to any living room. The chocolate brown yarn will add a touch of warmth and texture to neutral interiors, and you can add as many of the colourful popcorn stitches as you like.

# Popcorn-Stitch Cushion   Nicki Trench with Zara Poole

### MATERIALS
Debbie Bliss Cashmerino Chunky in the following shades and quantities:
  Six 50g balls shade 15 Chocolate Brown (Yarn A), two balls shade
  shade 11 Pale Blue (Yarn B), two balls shade 12 Pale Green (Yarn C)
7mm crochet hook
Tapestry needle
Mother-of-pearl button, approximately 3cm (1¼in) diameter
Round cushion pad 43cm (17 in) in diameter
Small pompom maker or cardboard to make template (see page 136)

### TENSION
Approximately 12tr = 10cm (4in).

### SPECIAL ABBREVIATIONS (See page 120 for standard abbreviations)
**pc – popcorn stitch:** Work 4 tr in the same place, slip the last loop off the hook. Reinsert the hook in the top of the first tr of the group and catch the empty loop. Pull this loop through to close the popcorn.

### CUSHION COVER
Make 2 sides. Work popcorns on front of cushion in Yarns B and C – alternate the rows of colour, pick up new colour on last pull-through of previous stitch. Work popcorns on back of cushion in Yarn A.
Using Yarn A make 6 ch and join with sl st to form a ring.
**Round 1:** 3 ch, 11 tr into ring, join with sl st to top of 3 ch.
**Round 2:** 3 ch, 1 tr in same st, * 2 tr into next st, repeat from * to end, join with sl st to top of 3 ch (24 sts).
**Round 3:** 3 ch, 1 tr in same st, * 1 tr in next st, 2 tr in next st twice, repeat from * to end, join with sl st to top of 3 ch (40 sts).
**Round 4:** 3 ch, 1 tr in same st, *1 tr in next 3 sts, 2 tr in next st, repeat from * to last 3 sts, 1 tr in last 3 sts, join with sl st to top of 3 ch (50 sts).
**Round 5:** 3 ch, 1 tr in same st, change to Yarn C and work * 1 pc in next st, change to Yarn A, 1 tr in next 4 sts, repeat from * to last 3 sts, 1 tr in next 3 sts, join with sl st to top of 3 ch.
**Round 6:** 3 ch, 1 tr in same st, *1 tr in next 5 sts, 2 tr in next st, repeat from * to last 6 sts, 1 tr in next 6 sts, join with sl st to top of 3 ch.
**Round 7:** 3 ch, 1 tr in same st, change to Yarn B and work * 1 pc in next st, change to Yarn A and work 1 tr in next 6 sts, repeat from *

to end, join with sl st to top of 3 ch.
**Round 8:** 3 ch, 1 tr in same st, * 1 tr in next 7 sts, 2 tr in next st, repeat from * to last 9 sts, 1 tr in next 9 sts, join with sl st to top of 3 ch.
**Round 9:** 3 ch, 1 tr in same st, * 1 tr in next 8 sts, change to Yarn C, 1 pc in next st, change to Yarn A, repeat from * to end, join with sl st to top of 3 ch.
**Round 10:** 3 ch, 1 tr in same st, * 1 tr in next 9 sts, 2 tr in next st, repeat from * to last 12 sts, 1 tr in next 12 sts, join with sl st to top of 3 ch.
**Round 11:** 3 ch, 1 tr in same st, 1 tr in next 6 sts, change to Yarn B, 1 pc in next st, change to Yarn A, 1 tr in next 10 sts, repeat from * to last 6 sts, 1 tr in next 6 sts, join with sl st to top of 3 ch.
**Round 12:** 3 ch, 1 tr in same st, * 1 tr in next 4 sts, 2 tr in next st, repeat from * to last 2 sts, 1 tr in next 2 sts, join with sl st to top of 3 ch. Fasten off.

### Central flower
With Yarn C make 6 ch.
**Round 1:** 3 ch (counts as 1st tr), * 2 ch, 1 tr into circle, rep from * 6 times, 2 ch, join with sl st to top of 3 ch.
**Round 2:** Into each 2-ch sp work (1 dc, 1 htr, 3 tr, 1 htr, 1 dc), join with sl st to sl st at end of round 1.
**Round 3:** * 4 ch, keeping chain behind petals of round 2, 1 dc into back of next tr on round 1, repeat from * 6 times, join with sl st to sl st at end of round 2.
**Round 4:** Into each 4-ch loop work (1 dc, 1 htr, 5 tr, 1 htr, 1 dc), join with sl st to sl st at end of round 3.
**Round 5:** As for round 3, working into the back of dc on round 3. Fasten off.
**Round 6:** Join Yarn C to sl st at end of last round. Into each 4-ch loop work (1 dc, 1 htr, 7 tr, 1 htr, 1 dc), join with sl st to sl st at end of round 5.
**Round 7:** As round 3, working into dc of round 5.
**Round 8:** Into each 4-ch loop work (1 dc, 1 htr, 2 tr, 5 dtr, 2 tr, 1 htr, 1 dc), join with sl st to sl st at end of round 7. Fasten off.
Sew in ends and sew flower on cushion. Sew button in centre of flower.

### FINISHING
Place wrong sides together and join with 1 row dc. Work two-thirds of the way round, insert cushion pad and continue rest of dc row. Fasten off. Make 10 pompoms, approx. 12cm (4¾in) diameter in a mixture of Yarn B and Yarn C and sew onto seam at regular intervals (see page 136).

This pretty shelf runner is the kind that would have graced the larders and kitchen dressers of our grandmothers and great-grandmothers. It is ideal for dressing up open shelves in modern kitchens and makes the perfect backdrop for an array of vintage china and kitchenware. Have fun embellishing it with a variety of buttons, charms or beads.

# Shelf Runner

## Emma Seddon

### MATERIALS
One 50g ball Blue Sky Alpacas Sportweight Baby Alpaca in each of the following shades: 500 Natural White (Yarn A), 47 Green (Yarn B)
Fabric the size of the shelf, plus 2cm (¾in) hem allowance around each edge
Buttons for decoration
3.5mm hook
Tapestry or chenille needle

### MEASUREMENTS
**Width of crochet edging:** 7cm (2¾in).

### TENSION
Obtaining a certain tension is not essential.

### ABBREVIATIONS
See page 120.

### SHELF RUNNER
Press under 2cm (¾in) along all edges of the fabric.
Using a tapestry or chenille needle and Yarn A, work blanket stitch along the edge of the fabric, keeping the stitches small and close together (see page 134).

### CROCHETED EDGES
**Row 1:** With RS towards you, join in Yarn A by double crocheting into each blanket-stitch loop. You need to end up with a multiple of 4 stitches, plus 1 to make repeat. You may need to dc into same space

twice to get the correct number of stitches. Fasten off.
**Row 2:** With RS towards you, join in Yarn B – make 4 ch, * miss 1 ch, 1 tr into next ch, 1 ch. Repeat from * all the way along. Fasten off.
**Row 3:** With WS towards you, join in Yarn A to first 1-ch space, 5 ch, tr into same space, * miss next 1-ch space, (1 tr, 2 ch, 1 tr) into next 1-ch space, rep from *. Turn.
**Row 4:** Sl st into 2-ch space, (2 dc, 3 ch, 2 dc) into same space, * sl st into space between trebles, (2 dc, 3 ch, 2 dc) into next 2-ch space. Repeat from *. Fasten off.
**Row 5:** With WS towards you, join in Yarn B to 3-ch space at end of point. 5 ch, tr into same space, * (1 tr, 2 ch, 1 tr) into next 3-ch space, rep from *. Turn.
**Row 6:** Repeat row 4.
**Row 7:** With RS facing, join in Yarn A to first dc, sl st into next ch, * (1 dc, 1 htr, 1 tr, 2 ch, 1 tr, 1 htr, 1 dc) into 3-ch space, sl st into next 2 chains, sl st into space between trebles, 3 ch, sl st back into space between trebles, sl st into next 2 chains. Repeat from *. Fasten off.

### FINISHING
Sew in ends using a tapestry needle.
Lay out shelf runner and place buttons (or beads, if you prefer) evenly over the crocheted edge of the runner.
To attach the buttons, first thread a separate length of Yarn A through each button, check that the button will face outwards when hanging by evening up the 2 ends of the yarn and holding each button up. Tie a knot at the top of the button to secure the yarn, and use the tapestry needle to sew the ends into the underside of the adjacent crochet stitches.

Decorated with clusters of exquisite Turkish 'Oya' needle-lace flowers attached at intervals along the bottom edge, this café curtain brings a quirky retro touch to any small window. It is attached at half height, making it ideal for use in a kitchen or bathroom, where it will offer some degree of privacy but still let in natural light. As an alternative trim, use crochet flowers, pompoms, fringe or buttons.

# Café Curtain

## Nicki Trench with Zara Poole

### MATERIALS
ggh Safari in the following quantities and shades: Four 50g balls shade 36 Green (Yarn A), one ball shade 41 Rust (Yarn B)
3mm crochet hook
Turkish 'Oya' needle-lace flowers (or other embellishments)
Needle and sewing thread

### MEASUREMENTS
60cm (24in) wide; 45cm (18in) deep.

### TENSION
3 complete shell repeats = approximately 10cm (4in).
Obtaining a certain tension is not essential.

### ABBREVIATIONS
See page 120.

### CURTAIN PANEL
Pattern worked using a basis of a multiple of 7 ch plus 2 ch, plus 2 ch on foundation row.
Using Yarn A make 116 ch.
**Row 1:** 1 tr in 4th ch from hook, * miss 2 ch, 5 tr in next ch, miss 2 ch, 1 tr in each of next 2 ch, repeat from * to end, turn.
**Row 2:** 3 ch, 2 tr in 1st tr, miss 3 tr, * 1 tr in space between 2nd and 3rd tr of group, 1 tr in sp between 3rd and 4th tr of group, miss 3 tr, 5 tr in sp between 2 vertical tr, miss 3 tr, repeat from *, ending 3 tr in sp between last tr and 3 ch, turn.
**Row 3:** 3 ch, 1 tr between 1st 2 tr, * miss 3 tr, 5 tr in space between 2 vertical tr, miss 3 tr, 1 tr in sp between 2nd and 3rd tr of group, 1 tr in sp between 3rd and 4th tr of group, repeat from *, ending 1 tr in sp between last tr and 3 ch, 1 tr in 3rd of 3 ch, turn.
Repeat rows 2 and 3 until work measures 45cm (18in). Fasten off.

### FINISHING
Finish off with a row of dc worked all the way round the top and sides in Yarn A and along the bottom in Yarn B.
Block following the instructions on page 137.
Use Yarn B to attach clusters of lace flowers (or other embellishment of your choice) at intervals.
Attach to window frame with decorative clips.

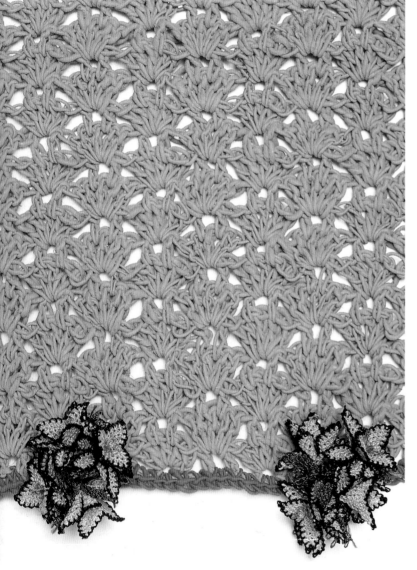

This funky lampshade, in a gorgeous combination of moose brown, burnt orange, rich gold and fir green, will add instant warmth, as well as a retro touch, to any room. It is made in sections, which means you can crochet as many or as few flowers as you need to cover your own style of shade. Sew the cover to the outside of an existing shade to limit the minimal risk of overheating.

# Twinkle Lampshade

## Claire Montgomerie

### MATERIALS
Blue Sky Alpacas Alpaca Silk in the following quantities and shades:
   Three 50g balls shade 130 Mandarin (Yarn A), five balls shade 131 Kiwi (Yarn B), three balls shade 132 Ginger (Yarn C), three balls shade 135 Chestnut (Yarn D)
4.5mm crochet hook
Lampshade: 20cm (8in) high, 30cm (12in) diameter
Chenille needle and strong matching thread

### TENSION
Flowers measure approximately 10cm (4in) diameter.
Obtaining a certain tension is not essential.

### ABBREVIATIONS
See page 120.

### FLOWERS
For the flowers, tie in the colours as randomly or as regularly as you wish, using a different colour for each visible round, keeping each flower one colour or a mixture. Here the flower colours are kept quite random, but generally use Yarn B (Kiwi) for the two lower base rounds, randomly swapping the remaining colours for the top two rounds.

Using the finger method (see page 127), make a ring for the centre of each flower. Wrap the yarn around two or three fingers (or a knitting needle of approximately 20mm) 20 times.
**Round 1:** Work 36 dc into ring made evenly so all wrapped yarn is covered. Join with sl st to 1st dc. Fasten off.

**Round 2:** Fasten in next colour. * 6 ch, miss 5 dc, 1 sl st into next dc, rep from * 5 times, ending with sl st into bottom of 1st ch (6 loops).
**Round 3:** * Work (1 dc, 2 htr, 11 tr, 2 htr, 1 dc) into 1st loop space, sl st to sl st, rep from * for next 5-ch loops. Fasten off yarn (6 petals).
**Round 4:** Attach next yarn and * work 6 ch, sl st into sl st of round 2, rep from * 5 times (6 loops).
**Round 5:** * Work (1 dc, 2 htr, 11 tr, 2 htr, 1 dc) into ch loop, sl st to sl st, rep from * for next 5-ch loops. Fasten off yarn (6 petals).
**Round 6:** Attach next yarn and * work 8 ch, sl st into sl st of round 2, rep from * 5 times (6 loops).
**Round 7:** * Work (1 dc, 2 htr, 15 tr, 2 htr, 1 dc) into ch loop, sl st to sl st, rep from * for next 5-ch loops. Fasten off yarn (6 petals).
**Round 8:** Still continuing in yarn used for round 7, attach yarn to a dc of round 1 that is inbetween the 2 sl sts of 1 petal from round 2, so that the next petals will be between the petals of previous rounds. * Work 10 ch, sl st into central dc between petal of round 2, rep from * 5 times more (6 loops).
**Round 9:** Work (1 dc, 2 htr, 19 tr, 2 htr, 1 dc) into ch loop, sl st to sl st, rep from * for next 5-ch loops. Fasten off yarn (6 petals).

Make enough flowers to cover your chosen lampshade as densely as you would like. Our shade required 30 flowers.

### FINISHING
To make up, sew all flowers together into a strip by the lowest layer of petals, joining by the central (10th) tr. Attach to lampshade either by sewing directly onto it using a chenille needle and matching thread or by making 3 ch at the top and 3 ch at the bottom and then tying them on the inside of the shade.

The subtle pastel colours of sugared almonds inspired this adorable breakfast set of cosies to keep tea, coffee and boiled eggs warm. The ritual of a traditional family breakfast is a lovely way to wake up and start the day, especially on lazy weekends.

# Kate's Breakfast Set

**Kate Samphier**

## MATERIALS

### For tea cosy

One 50g ball Blue Sky Alpacas Sportweight in each of the following
    shades: 514 Pale Aqua (Yarn A), 506 Natural Streaky Brown (Yarn B)
5mm crochet hook

### For cafetière cosy

One 50g ball Blue Sky Alpacas Sportweight in each of the following
    shades: 515 Pistachio (Yarn A), 506 Natural Streaky Brown (Yarn B)
    (for contrast picot trim)
4.5mm crochet hook
3 vintage buttons, approximately 3cm (1¼in) diameter
Needle and sewing thread

### For egg cosies

One 50g ball Blue Sky Alpacas Sportweight in each of the following
    shades (for 6 cosies, 2 in each colour): 505 Natural Taupe (Yarn A),
    514 Pale Aqua (Yarn B), 500 Natural White (Yarn C); (for contrast
    picot trim) one ball shade 506 Natural Streaky Brown (Yarn D)
4.5mm crochet hook
One vintage button for each cosy, 10-15mm (½-⅝in) diameter
Needle and thread

## MEASUREMENTS

**Tea cosy:** 14cm (5½in) deep; 20cm (8in) diameter at rim (fits average
small teapot).
**Cafetière cosy:** 13cm (5in) deep; 30cm (12in) long (fits standard 1 litre
or 6 cup cafetière).
**Egg cosy:** 6cm (2½in) deep, 8cm (3in) diameter at bottom edge.

## TENSION

For tea cosy: 1 motif = 3cm (1¼in), using 5mm crochet hook.
Using 4.5mm hook, 17 st = 10cm (4in).

## ABBREVIATIONS

See page 120.

## TEA COSY

Using Yarn B and 5mm hook, make 32 ch.
**Row 1:** 1 dc in 2nd ch from hook, 1 dc in each ch to end. 31 sts.
Change to Yarn A.
**Row 2 (WS):** 3 ch, * miss 3 sts, 3 tr in next st, (group made); rep from
* to last 3 sts, miss 2 sts, 1 tr in last st.
**Row 3:** 1 ch, 1 dc in first st, 2 tr in next free st of 2 rows below
(working round sts of previous row), * 1 dc in centre of group of 3 tr,
3 tr in centre of 3 free sts, of 2 rows below; rep from * ending 1 dc in

centre tr of last group, 2 tr in centre of 3 free sts, 1 dc in top of 3 ch.
**Row 4:** Repeat row 1.
**Row 5:** Repeat row 2.
**Rows 6-14:** Repeat rows 2-5 twice more, then row 1 again.
**Row 15:** 1 ch, 1 dc in first st, 2 tr in next free st, * 1 dc in centre tr of
next group 2 tr in centre free st, rep from * to end, 1 dc in top of 3 ch.
Change to Yarn B
**Row 16:** 3 ch, * miss 1 st, dec 1; rep from * ending 1 tr in last st.
**Row 17:** 3 ch, * dec 1; rep from * ending 1 tr in top of 3 ch. Fasten off.
Make another piece the same.

Join seams (see page 137), leaving openings for spout and handle.

## CAFETIÈRE COSY

Using Yarn A make 49 ch.
**Row 1:** Work in dc.
Continue to work rows of dc until work measures 11cm (4½in) from
starting edge. Fasten off.

### Picot edge

Join in Yarn B and, working into loops from previous row, * 3 ch, 1 dc
in first of these ch, miss 1 st, 1 dc in next st; rep from * to end. Fasten off.
Turn work to bottom edge and join in Yarn B, and work picot edge to
match above. Fasten off.

### Button loops

Using Yarn B work 3 button loops in ch, to the size appropriate for
your chosen buttons. Stitch onto edge of cosy.
Using needle and thread, sew buttons along opposite edge to
correspond with button loops.

## EGG COSY (Make 2 cosies in each of Yarns A, B and C)

Using Yarn A make 3 ch, join into ring with slip stitch.
**Round 1:** 6 dc into ring.
**Round 2:** (2 dc in each st) 6 times (12 sts).
**Round 3:** (1 dc in next st, 2 dc in next st) 6 times (18 sts).
**Round 4:** (1 dc in each of next 2 sts, 2 dc in next st) 6 times (24 sts).
**Rounds 5-7:** Work 5 rounds dc.
**Round 8:** Change to contrast Yarn D, * 3 ch, 1 dc in first of these ch,
miss 1 st, 1 dc in next st; rep from * to end. Fasten off.
Repeat to make another cosy in Yarn A, then make 4 more cosies
using Yarn B and Yarn C.

Using a needle and thread sew vintage button to top of cosy.

Lazy Summers

Vintage-style patterned cotton fabric ripped into strips and used instead of conventional yarn has given this picnic blanket tons of character, as well as making it strong and functional. The edging has been worked in a natural linen yarn, which adds to the rustic appeal. On the next sunny day, roll up the blanket, pack up your hamper and head for the nearest meadow, beach or park— or take it on camping trips.

# Picnic Blanket

## Bee Clinch

### MATERIALS
Three 400g 'cheese' Texere Natural Pure Linen Fancy, shade
  Silver & White
9m/10yd cotton fabric, torn into twenty 2mm (1⁄16in) strips and the
  rest into 3mm (1⁄8in) strips
5.5mm and 15mm crochet hooks
Tapestry needle

### MEASUREMENTS
**Inner square:** 62 x 62cm (24½ x 24½in).
**Finished blanket:** 132 x 132cm (52 x 52in).

### TENSION
Using the 5.5mm hook and linen yarn, each square should measure
33 x 33cm (13 x 13in). With the 15mm hook and 3mm (1⁄8in) fabric
strips, 4sts over 10cm (4in).

### ABBREVIATIONS
See page 120.

### SPECIAL ABBREVIATIONS
**frtr – front raised treble (also known as 'cable stitch':** Yarn over
hook and insert from front to back around post of next dc 2nd round
down, draw up a 1cm (½in) loop, yrh and pull through 2 loops twice.

### NOTES
Depending on your preference, the size of the blanket can be
increased by adding more squares and adapting the size of the
central fabric square. More yarn and fabric will have to be purchased
according to the size you wish to make.

**To make fabric strips:** Tear down the length of the fabric at 3mm
(1⁄8in) intervals to create fabric 'yarn' (make a small cut with scissors
to start you off). In the same way, tear 20 strips 2mm (1⁄16in) wide for
the contrast rounds in the square motif.

### LINEN SQUARE MOTIF (Make 12)
With linen yarn and 5.5mm hook, ch 4, join with sl st into ring.
**Round 1:** Ch 1, 8 dc into ring, join in 1st dc with sl st. Turn.
Turn at end of every round.
**Round 2:** Ch 1, 1 dc in joined stitch, 1 dc in next dc, * (corner group of
1 dc, ch 2, 1 dc) in next dc, 1 dc in next dc, repeat from * around; sl st
in 1st dc (3 sts per side).
**Round 3:** Ch 1, 1 dc in joining dc, 1 dc in each st to ch-2 sp at corner, *
a corner group in ch-2 sp, 1 dc in each st to next ch-2 sp, repeat from
* around; sl st in 1st dc (5 sts per side).
**Rounds 4-9:** Repeat round 3 six times (17 sts per side).
Fasten off.
**Round 10:** With 2mm (1⁄16in) fabric strip and 5mm hook, ch 1, work 1 dc
in joining dc; continue as in round 3 but change back to linen yarn in
last dc (19 sts per side).

**Round 11 (RS):** Continuing in linen yarn, ch 1, 1 dc in joining dc, * 1 dc in each of next 5 dc, frtr in next dc, 1 dc in each of next 7 dc, work a frtr st, 1 dc in each of next 5 dc, a corner group in next ch-2 sp, repeat from * around omitting corner group from last repeat; sl st in 1st dc (21 sts per side).

**Round 12:** Repeat round 3 (23 sts per side).

**Round 13:** Ch 1, 1 dc in joining dc, * 1 dc in each of next 7 dc, frtr around cable stitch below, 1 dc in each of next 7 dc, frtr around cable stitch below, 1 dc in each of next 7 dc, a corner group in ch-2 sp: repeat from * around, ending and joining as before (25 sts per side).

**Round 14:** Repeat round 3 (27 sts per side).

**Round 15:** Ch 1, 1 dc in joining dc, * 1 dc in each of next 9 dc, frtr as before, 1 dc in each of next 7 dc, frtr as before, 1 dc in each of next 9 dc, a corner group in ch-2 sp: repeat from * around, ending and joining as before. Fasten off.

Make 11 more squares.

## CENTRAL FABRIC SQUARE

Using 3mm (⅛in) fabric strip and 15mm hook, ch 30 + 1. Turn.

**Row 1:** Dc in 2nd st from hook, continue in dc to end. Ch 1, turn.

Repeat row 1 until work measures 66cm (26in).

## FINISHING

Join the linen square motifs together with dc, forming a frame shape with 4 squares along each side.

Join frame to central fabric square with dc.

Sew in loose ends. Press.

Now pack your hamper and fill your flask!

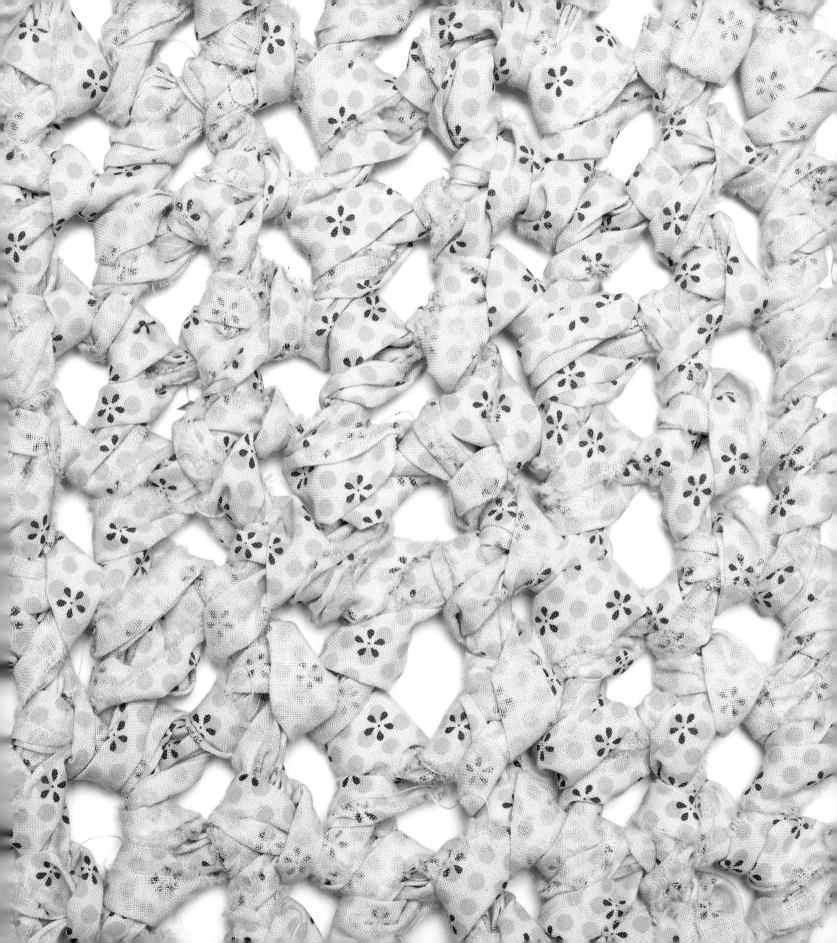

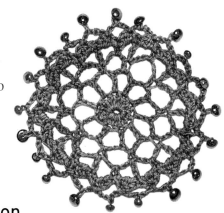

Keep the bugs and falling leaves out of your dishes of food and jugs of drinks when you're eating outdoors with this great selection of covers for jars, bowls, glasses and jugs. This project provides a great opportunity to make samples and try out new stitches on a small scale. Embellish to your heart's desire with vintage buttons or charms to weight the covers down.

# Assortment of Covers — Emma Seddon

## MATERIALS

One 50g ball Be Sweet Bamboo in each of the following shades:
  645 Pale Lilac (Yarn A), 644 Dark Lilac (Yarn B), 613 Deep Orange
  (Yarn C), 627 Celery (Yarn D), 655 Shell Pink (Yarn E)
4mm crochet hook
Selection of small buttons, 1–2cm (½–¾in) diameter (see individual
  patterns for number required)
Tapestry needle

## MEASUREMENTS

**Sugar bowl cover:** 14cm (5½in) diameter.
**Fruit bowl cover:** 25cm (10in) diameter.
**Beaker cover:** 16cm (6½in) diameter.
**Milk jug cover:** 23cm (9in) diameter.
**Salad bowl cover:** 33cm (13in) diameter.

## TENSION

Obtaining a certain tension is not essential.

## ABBREVIATIONS

See page 120

## SUGAR BOWL COVER (Above right)

Using Yarn A thread on 20 assorted buttons.
Using 4mm hook make slip loop, 4 ch, join with sl st into circle.
**Round 1:** 3 ch, 10 tr into circle, join with sl st into circle.
**Round 2:** 6 ch, 1 tr into next chain after sl st, * 3 ch, 1 tr into next chain, repeat from *, 3 ch, sl st into 3rd ch of 6 ch at beg of round.
**Round 3:** Sl st into next 3-ch space, 1 dc into same space, * 5 ch, 1 dc in next 3-ch space, rep from *, 5 ch, sl st into 1st dc.
**Round 4:** 2 ch, sl st into next 5-ch space, 1 dc into same space, * 3 ch, 1 tr into top of dc (on row below), 3 ch, 1 dc into centre of 5-ch space, rep from *, 3 ch, 1 tr into dc (on row below), 3 ch, sl st into 1st dc.

**Round 5:** (1 htr, 1 tr, 1 htr) into same 3-ch space as sl st, * sl st into tr on previous row, (1 htr, 1 tr, 1 htr) into next 3-ch space, sl st into dc on previous round, repeat from *, sl st into 1st dc.
**Round 6:** Sl st along next 2 st, (you'll be above the tr), * 3 ch, push button into position, 2 ch, sl st into tr at centre of next scallop, repeat from *, 3 ch, push button into position, 2 ch, sl st into space at start of round. Fasten off and sew in ends.

## FRUIT BOWL COVER (Opposite centre)

Using Yarn B thread on 17 buttons
Using 4mm hook make 4 ch, join with sl st into a circle.
**Round 1:** 5 ch (counts as 1 tr, 2 ch), * 1 tr, 2 ch, repeat from * 6 times, join with sl st to 3rd ch of 5 ch at beg of round.
**Round 2:** Sl st into 1st 2-ch sp, 3 ch, 2 tr in same sp, * 3 tr into each 2-ch space, repeat from *, sl st to top of 1st tr.
**Round 3:** 6 ch, (1 tr in each of next 3 ch, working only 1st 2 loops on each st and holding remaining loops on hook, yrh and pull through all 4 loops on hook = 1 cluster made), * 3 ch, 1 tr between clusters, 3 ch, work 1 cluster, repeat from *, 3 ch, sl st into 3rd ch of 6 ch at beg of round.
**Round 4:** Sl st into 1st space, dc into same space, * 6 ch, 1 dc into next 3-ch space, repeat from *, 6 ch, sl st to 1st dc.
**Round 5:** Sl st along 1st 3 ch of 6 ch, 1 dc into same 6-ch space, * 6 ch, 1 dc into next 6-ch space, repeat from *, 6 ch, sl st into 1st dc.
**Round 6:** Sl st along 1st 3 ch of 6 ch, 1 dc into same 6-ch space, * 7 ch, 1 dc into next 6-ch space, repeat from *, 7 ch, sl st into 1st dc.
**Round 7:** Sl st along 1st 3 ch of 7 ch, 1 dc into same 7-ch space, * 7 ch, 1 dc into next 7-ch space, 7 ch, sl st to 1st dc.
**Round 8:** Sl st along 1st 3 ch of 7 ch, 1 dc into same 7-ch space, * 8 ch, 1 dc in next 7-ch space, * 8 ch, sl st into 1st dc.
**Round 9:** Sl st along 1st 4 ch of 8 ch, 1 dc into same 8-ch space, * 8 ch, 1 dc into next 8-ch space, repeat from * 8 ch, sl st into 1st dc.
**Round 10:** Turn, with WS towards you, 2 ch, push button into position, 3 ch, sl st back to sl st at end of last round, * (3 ch, miss 2 ch, sl st

into next ch, 3 ch, miss 2 ch, sl st into next ch, 3 ch, miss 2 ch) along 8 ch, sl st into dc in between 8-ch spaces, 2 ch, push button into place, 3 ch, sl st back into same dc, repeat from * to end, (3 ch, miss 2 ch, sl st into next ch, 3 ch, miss 2 ch, 3 ch, miss 2 ch) along 8 ch, sl st into 1st dc.

Fasten off and sew in ends.

### BEAKER COVER (Below)

Using Yarn C thread on 22 assorted buttons.

Using 4mm hook make 5 ch, join with sl st into a circle.

**Round 1:** 1 ch, 14 dc into circle, join with sl st to 1st dc.

**Round 2:** 2 ch, 1 tr in same space pulling through 1st 2 loops, (leaving 2 loops on hook), (work 2 tr, by pulling through 1st 2 loops on each st, leaving last loop on hook) into next ch, (4 loops on hook), yrh and pull through all 4 loops, * 3 ch, (2 tr, pull through 1st 2 loops on each st, leaving last loop on hook) into next 2 ch, (5 loops on hook), yrh and pull through all 5 loops, (1 cluster made), repeat from * 6 times, 3 ch, sl st to top of 1st cluster.

**Round 3:** Sl st into next 3-ch space, 4 dc into same 3-ch space, * 4 dc into next 3-ch space, repeat from *, join with sl st into 1st dc.

**Round 4:** 5 ch, * 1 dtr in next dc, 1 ch, repeat from *, sl st into 4th ch of 5 ch at beginning of round.

**Round 5:** 2 ch, 1 tr in same space as sl st, * 3 ch, miss next 1 ch, work sl st, 3 ch, miss 2 sts (work 3 tr, working 1st 2 loops of each st, and leaving last loops on hook, yrh and pull through all 4 loops on hook = 1 cluster worked), repeat from * 3 ch, miss 1 ch, sl st in next ch, 3 ch, sl st in top of 1st tr.

**Round 6:** * 4 ch, work 1 cluster in same place as sl st worked between clusters on previous round, 4 ch, sl st in top of next cluster on previous round, repeat from * 4 ch, work 1 cluster in same place as sl st worked between clusters on previous round, 4 ch, sl st into same place as 1st sl st on round.

**Round 7:** Turn work with WS facing and work 1 ch, * (1 dc in next 4-ch sp, 2 ch, push button into place, 3 ch, 1 dc in same 4-ch sp, 1 ch), repeat from *, sl st to 1st dc in round. Fasten off and sew in ends.

### MILK JUG COVER (Opposite top)

Using Yarn D thread on 29 mother-of-pearl buttons.

Using 4mm hook make 4 ch, join with sl st into circle, 1 ch.

**Round 1:** 10 dc into circle, join with sl st into a circle.

**Round 2:** 4 ch, * 1 tr into next dc, 1 ch, repeat from *, sl st into 3rd ch of 4 ch at beginning of round.

**Round 3:** 5 ch, * miss 1 ch, 1 tr into top of next tr of round below, 2 ch, repeat from *, sl st into 3rd ch of 5 ch at beginning of round.

**Round 4:** Sl st into 1st 2-ch space, 4 dc into each 2-ch space, sl st into 1st dc.

**Round 5:** 4 ch, * 1 tr into next dc, 1 ch, rep from *, join with sl st to 3rd ch of 4 ch at beg of round.

**Round 6:** 3 ch, tr into same space as sl st, 2 ch, * miss 2 sts, (make 1 tr, leaving 2 loops on hook, make another tr into same space, pull hook through all 3 loops at once = 1 cluster), 2 ch, repeat from *, join with sl st to top of 1st cluster.

**Round 7:** Sl st into next 2-ch space, 2 ch, 1 tr in same 2-ch space, * 3 ch, make 1 cluster in next 2-ch space, repeat from *, 3 ch, sl st into top of 1st cluster.

**Round 8:** Sl st into next 3-ch space, 2 ch, 2 tr into same 3-ch space, (working only the 1st 2 loops of each tr, leaving other loops on hook, yrh, pull hook through all 3 loops), * 3 ch, (3 tr, pulling loop through 1st 2 loops of each st, holding remaining loops on hook, yrh, hook through all 4 loops = 1 cluster) in each 3-ch space, repeat from *, 3 ch, sl st into top of 1st cluster.

**Round 9:** * 6 ch, push button into place, 1 ch, sl st back along 2 ch before button, 4 ch, sl st into top of next cluster, repeat from *, finish last repeat by sl st into same place as round started.

Fasten off and sew in ends.

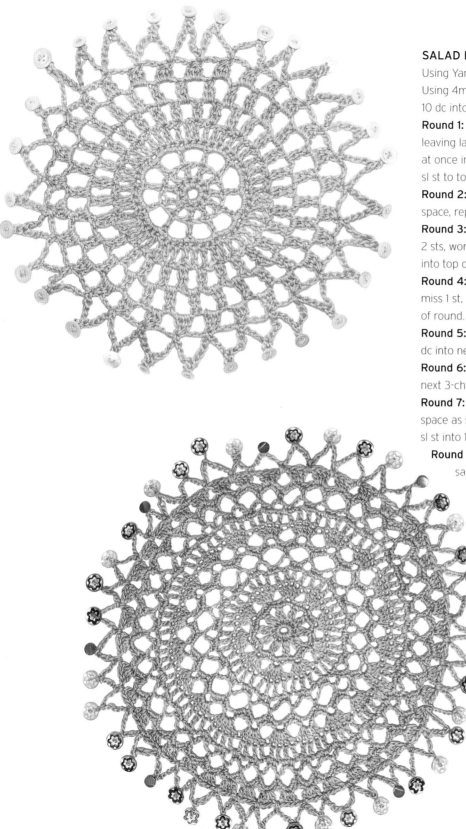

## SALAD BOWL COVER (Below)

Using Yarn E thread on 43 buttons.

Using 4mm hook make 4 ch, join with sl st into circle, 1 ch.

10 dc into circle, join with sl st into a circle.

**Round 1:** 3 ch, 1 tr into space where sl st just made, * 2 ch, (work 1 tr, leaving last 2 loops on hook, work next tr and pull through all 3 loops at once in next ch = 1 cluster worked), repeat from *, 2 ch, join with sl st to top of 3 ch at beginning of round.

**Round 2:** Sl st along tops of chains to 2-ch space, * 3 dc into 2-ch space, repeat from * to end of round, sl st into top of 1st dc made.

**Round 3:** Sl st into next st, 3 ch, 4 tr into same space as sl st, * miss 2 sts, work 5 tr into next ch (centre dc of 3 dcs), repeat from *, sl st into top of 1st 3 ch.

**Round 4:** 4 ch, * (1 tr into next st, 1 ch) 3 times, 1 tr into next st, miss 1 st, repeat from * to end, sl st into 3rd ch of 4 ch at beginning of round.

**Round 5:** 1 ch, dc into next 1-ch space, * 3 ch, dc into next 1-ch space, dc into next 1-ch space, repeat from *, 3 ch, sl st into 1st dc.

**Round 6:** Sl st into next 3-ch loop, dc into same space, * 4 ch, dc into next 3-ch loop, repeat from *, 4 ch, sl st into 1st dc.

**Round 7:** Sl st into next 4-ch space, (2 dc, 3 ch, 2 dc) into same 4-ch space as sl st, * (2 dc, 3 ch, 2 dc) into next 4-ch space, repeat from * sl st into 1st dc.

**Round 8:** Sl st along top of next 2 sts to 3-ch space, 3 ch, 4 tr into same 3-ch space as sl st, * 5 tr in next 3-ch space, repeat from * sl st into top of 1st 3 ch.

**Round 9:** 4 ch, * (1 tr into next ch, 1 ch) 3 times, 1 tr in next ch, miss 1 ch, repeat from *, sl st in top of 3rd ch of 4 ch at beginning of round.

**Round 10:** Repeat round 5.

**Round 11:** Repeat round 6.

**Round 12:** Sl st into next 4-ch space, (2 dc, 1 ch, 2 dc) into same 4-ch space as sl st, * (2 dc, 1 ch, 2 dc) into next 4-ch space, repeat from *, sl st into 1st dc.

**Round 13:** Sl st along top of next 2 sts to 1-ch space, 3 ch, 3 tr into same 1-ch space as sl st, * 4 tr in next 1-ch space, repeat from *, sl st into top of 3 ch at beginning of round.

**Round 14:** * 4 ch, push button into place, 5 ch, 1 dc into space between 4 trs of previous row, repeat from *. Fasten off and sew in ends.

This pretty shell-stitch tablecloth is perfect for alfresco breakfast, lunch or tea. Crocheted balls filled with small weights are attached at each corner and along the edges of the cloth, to help prevent it from flying away in the breeze. The crocheted balls are echoed by the jaunty polkadot design, worked in alternating blue and green.

# Garden Tablecloth

## Nicki Trench with Zara Poole

### MATERIALS
Debbie Bliss Cotton DK in the following quantities and shades:
   Twenty-three 50g balls shade 02 Cream (Yarn A)
   Two balls shade 20 Green (Yarn B)
   Two balls shade 09 Blue (Yarn C)
7mm crochet hook
12 small weights, such as ball bearings

### MEASUREMENTS
112 x 92cm (44 x 36in).

### TENSION
Yarn tension: 20 stitches to 4 inches (10cm) and 28 rows.
Obtaining a certain tension is not essential.

### ABBREVIATIONS
See page 120.

### NOTE
The size may be adapted by using more or less chain at the beginning, as long as it is worked in multiples of 6 + 1, and working more or less rows.

### TABLECLOTH
Make 92 ch.
**Row 1:** 1 dc in 2nd ch from hook, * miss 2 ch, 5 tr in next ch (shell made), miss 2 ch, 1 dc in next ch, repeat from * ending with 1 dc in last ch, turn.

**Row 2:** 3 ch, 2 tr in 1st st (half shell) * 1 dc in centre tr of shell on previous row, work 5 tr in next dc, repeat from * ending with 3 tr in last dc, turn.

**Row 3:** 1 ch, 1 dc in 1st tr * work 5 tr in next dc, 1 dc in centre tr of next shell, repeat from * ending with 1 dc in top 3 ch, turn.

Repeat rows 2 and 3 until 60 rows have been worked, placing dots as described below.

Fasten off.

### Working the coloured dots

Dots are worked in Yarn B and Yarn C over 3 rows; pick up new colour on last pull-through of previous stitch.

**Row 1 of dot:** Work a 5-tr shell.

**Row 2 of dot:** Work the 3 tr either side of shell on previous row.

**Row 3 of dot:** Work the 5-tr shell as above in row 1.

Place the dots as follows:

**Rows 9, 29 and 49:** Start the dot on the 4th, 8th and 12th shells.

**Rows 19 and 39:** Start the dot on the 5th and 10th shells.

Alternate the colours of the dots on each row.

### EDGING

Worked in Yarn A all around the tablecloth starting at one corner:
* 1 dc in edge, miss 2 st, make 5 tr in next st, miss 2 st, repeat from * all round and sl st to join.

### CROCHET BALLS (Make 4 in each colour – 12 in total)

Make 3 ch, join with sl st to form a ring.

**Row 1:** 3 ch, 12 tr into ring, join with sl st to top of 3 ch.

**Row 2:** 1 ch, 1 dc in each st, sl st to join.

**Rows 3 and 4:** Repeat row 2.

Fasten off, leaving a tail of about 10cm (4in).

Using a tapestry needle, weave this tail through the tops of all the stitches on the last row.

Stuff ball with scraps of same colour yarn, insert weight into centre and draw up tight.

### FINISHING

To attach the balls, use Yarn A to make 15 ch and fasten off, leaving a tail of about 10cm (4in).

Knot the 2 loose ends together to make a ring and tie securely to the loose end of the crochet ball. Tidy the loose ends inside the crochet ball. Repeat for the 11 other balls.

Attach the balls to the tablecloth (1 on each corner and 2 spaced equally along each side) by inserting the ch loop through the middle of an edge shell and pushing the crochet ball through the loop.

This amazing tent can be staked to the ground or slung over the branches of a tree to create a picnic 'camp'. Alternatively, suspend it on ropes over an outdoor dining table to make a gorgeous garden canopy. Decorate it with crocheted flowers or weave outdoor fairy lights through the net to make it even more magical and romantic.

# Papillon Canopy    Leigh Radford

### MATERIALS

Rowan Bamboo Tape in the following quantities and shades:
  Twenty-one 50g balls shade 711 Antique Rose (Yarn A)
  Ten balls shade 705 Wafer (Yarn B)
4mm, 5mm and 9mm crochet hooks, or hooks needed to obtain
  correct tension
Chenille needle (with a sharp point)
Approximately 24m (79ft) of 9mm (⅜in) manila rope

### MEASUREMENTS

Approximately 3.15m (10¼ft) long; 2.9m (9½ft) wide.

### TENSION

Using a 9mm crochet hook, each diamond (from one knot to the next) will be about 7cm (2¾in) wide; however, obtaining a certain tension is not crucial.

### ABBREVIATIONS

See page 120.

### SPECIAL ABBREVIATIONS

**sk – Solomon's knot:** See page 130.

### MAIN PANELS (Make 5)

With 9mm hook and Yarn A, ch 1 drawing up loop to approximately 4.5cm (1¾in). Wrap the yarn over the hook, drawing the loop on the hook through, keeping the single back thread of this long chain separate from the 2 front threads. Insert the hook under this single back thread and wrap the yarn again. Draw a loop through and wrap again. Draw through both loops on the hook. Ch 1. One sk is completed. Repeat until you have completed 18 sks.

**Row 1:** Turn work and ch 1 in 3rd knot from hook drawing up loop to 4.5cm (1¾in). Repeat steps above, creating 2 sk. * Miss one knot from previous row and work 1 dc in next knot. Repeat from * across to end. Work 2 'end knots' drawing up loops only 3.5cm (1½in) (instead of 4.5cm/1¾in).
Work all rows as for row 1, working even until panel measures approximately 315cm (124in) long.

### DIVIDERS (Make 6)

With 5mm hook and Yarn B, ch 325.
**Row 1:** Change to 4mm hook and beg with 3rd ch from hook, work 1 tr in each ch to end of row (325 tr). Ch 2, turn.
**Row 2:** 1 tr in each tr of previous row to end. Fasten off.
Weave in ends. (The dividers will be slightly shorter than the main panels.)

### RINGS (Make 54)

With 5mm hook and yarn B, ch 9. Insert hook into 1st ch and join with sl st. Ch 1. Work 13 dc in centre of ring. Insert hook into the top of the starting chain and make a sl st to join. Cut, leaving a tail approximately 7.5cm (3in).

## FINISHING

Lay all the main panels side by side on a flat surface, as shown in the diagram below. Lay one divider on top of the outside edge of the first main panel (slightly overlapping the edges). Pin one end of the divider to the top corner of the panel and pin the opposite end of the divider to the bottom corner of the panel, stretching the divider to fit. (Making the dividers shorter than the main panels and stretching them into place results in a sturdier piece of fabric, once the entire canopy has been assembled). Pin the entire divider along the edge/length of the main panel.

Cut a 6m (20ft) strand of Yarn B. Thread through chenille needle and pull flush with opposite end, dividing overall length to 3m (3¼ yards) (double strand). Beginning at lower right corner, insert threaded needle into wrong side of divider and sew divider to panel using whip stitch, removing pins as you work.

Repeat for each panel until entire canopy is assembled.

Working on wrong side of canopy, position rings at either end of first divider and every 35cm (13¾in) in between (you will have nine rings per dividing panel. Thread 7.5cm (3in) tail from ring through needle and sew base of ring to divider, using whip stitch, until securely fastened.

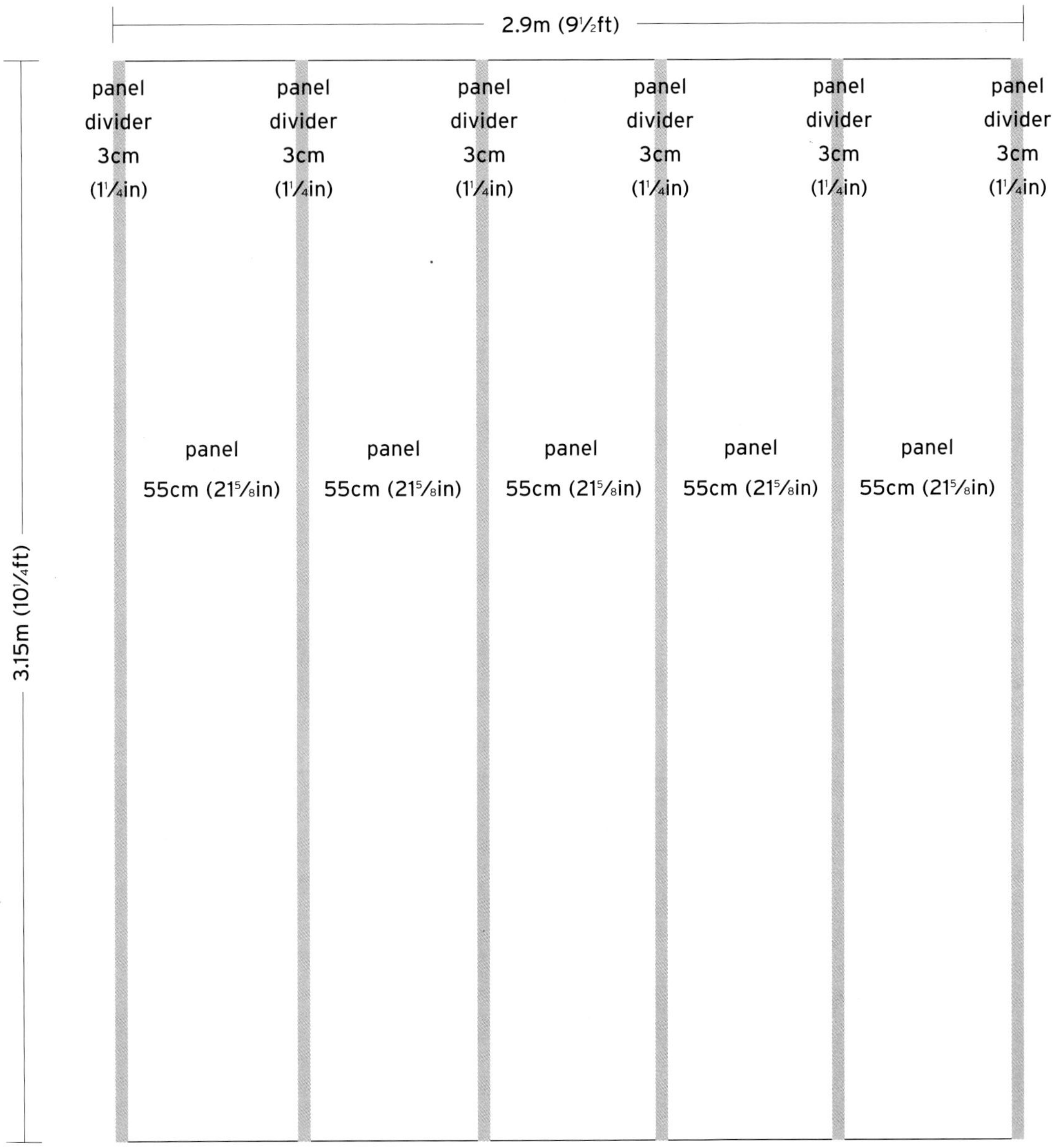

2.9m (9½ft)

| panel divider 3cm (1¼in) | panel divider 3cm (1¼in) | panel divider 3cm (1¼in) | panel divider 3cm (1¼in) | panel divider 3cm (1¼in) | panel divider 3cm (1¼in) |

3.15m (10¼ft)

| panel 55cm (21⅝in) | panel 55cm (21⅝in) | panel 55cm (21⅝in) | panel 55cm (21⅝in) | panel 55cm (21⅝in) |

Here is a great catch-all bag to sling over your shoulders and carry your essentials, from magazine or book to sunglasses and water bottle – perfect for shopping, days out, picnics or going to the beach. The mouthwatering burnt-orange yarn is like a burst of summer sunshine and will make you feel happy even if the sky is cloudy. Customize your bag by using some gorgeous wide ribbon for the shoulder strap.

# Hipster Tote

## Bee Clinch

### MATERIALS

Eight 50g balls ggh Big Easy, shade 3 Burnt Orange
5mm crochet hook
1m (1yd) fabric for lining
3m (3¼yds) linen ribbon, 5cm (2in) wide
Tapestry needle
Sewing machine
Sewing needle
Matching sewing thread
Piece of strong cardboard, at least 30 x 9cm (12 x 3½in)

### MEASUREMENTS

36cm (14in) deep; approximately 30cm (12in) wide at bottom.

### TENSION

13 sts over 10cm (4in) using 5mm hook.

### ABBREVIATIONS

See page 120.

## SPECIAL ABBREVIATIONS

**ps – puff stitch:** Yarn round hook, insert into stitch and pull up loop (approximately 2cm/¾in), yarn round hook, insert into same stitch and pull up loop to same length as previous. Repeat this process 4 times in total (9 loops), yarn round hook and pull through all loops on hook. Close puff stitch made with 1 chain.

**dc into back loop:** Dc in the usual manner but into the back loop of the stitch only.

## FRONT AND BASE

Ch 30 + 1.

**Row 1:** Dc into 2nd ch from hook. Dc to end. Ch 1, turn.
**Row 2:** Dc into back loop of next st, repeat to end. Ch 1, turn.
Repeat row 2 for 12 rows in total.

Now proceed in puff-stitch pattern.
**Row 1:** Dc to end. Ch 2, turn.
**Row 2:** Ps into 1st st, repeat to end (30 ps in total). Ch 1, turn.
Repeat row 1 but only dc into top stitch of ps and not the stitch between. This sets the pattern.
Repeat rows 1 and 2 eleven times each.
**Next row:** Dc to end.

### To form the base panel

**Row 1:** Sl st 3 st, dc to last 3 st (25 sts). Ch 1, turn.
**Row 2:** Dc into next dc 2 rows below. Continue dc into all stitches 2 rows below. Ch 1, turn.
Repeat rows 1 and 2 for 10 rows. Fasten off.

## BACK

Complete as for front, omitting base panel.

## FINISHING

With wrong sides together, match base panel to back piece, making sure that there is a 3-st difference either side.
Either sew the two pieces together or dc tog.
Sew or crochet the front and back side seams together along the ps rows and ridged top facing only, leaving the bottom seams open.
Match the sewn side seam to centre of base section and sew together.
Complete for other side.

### Reinforced base

Ch 40 + 1. Turn.
**Row 1:** Dc in 2nd ch from hook, dc to end. Ch 1, turn.
Continue in dc until piece measures 14cm (5½in). Fasten off.

Fold piece in half and dc tog round 2 sides.
Cut a piece of strong card to fit inside and slip in. Dc closed and then place in bottom of bag to fit into base section.

### Ribbon handle

Fold ribbon in half and adjust to length required. Sew together along both sides of ribbon. Sew each end securely at side seams at 2nd and 3rd ps row.

### Fabric lining

**1.** Cut two pieces of lining fabric, for front and back of bag, each measuring 38 x 43cm (15 x 17in) wide. Cut one piece of lining fabric for the base, measuring 34 x 11cm (13½ x 4½in).
**2.** Place the front and back panels together with right sides facing and machine stitch the side seams. Finish the raw edges with zigzag stitch or make a French seam to enclose raw edges. (To make a French seam, first sew the seam with wrong sides facing, trim and press, then sew the seam with right sides facing so the raw edges are enclosed.)
**3.** With right sides facing, insert the base panel, matching the sewn side seams to the center of the shorter sides of the base panel; pin then machine stitch. Finish raw edges as above.
**4.** Press under a 1cm (½in) hem along top edge. Turn lining rightside out and press.
**5.** Place lining in crochet bag and slipstitch to inside of bag where ridged facing joins first ps row, being sure to cover ribbon ends.

Gorgeous Gifts

Made with pear tree's yummy ultra-soft merino yarn in colours that remind us of old-fashioned pyjamas faded with wear, this beautiful blanket feels almost as good as cashmere. It makes the perfect gift for a newborn baby and is sure to be treasured for years to come – or, you may think it's so divine that you'll want to keep going and size it up for your own bed.

# Baby Blanket of Roses

## Kate Samphier

### MATERIALS
pear tree 8-ply Merino in the following quantities and shades:
   Three 50g balls shade Moss
   One ball in each of the following shades: Blush, Grass, Ecru,
   Robin's Egg
5mm crochet hook
Small pompom maker or cardboard to make pompom template
   (see page 136)
Tapestry needle

### Colour combination 1
Yarn A - Ecru
Yarn B - Robin's Egg
Yarn C - Moss

### Colour combination 2
Yarn A - Ecru
Yarn B - Blush
Yarn C - Moss

### Double-knot stitch embroidery
Yarn D - Grass

### MEASUREMENTS
Approximately 50 x 70cm (20 x 28in).

### TENSION
14 stitches per 10cm (4in) worked in pattern.

## ABBREVIATIONS

See page 120.

## NOTE

By increasing the number of squares, you can increase the dimensions of your blanket.

## BLANKET

Using 5mm hook work 8 squares in colour combination 1 and another 7 squares in colour combination 2 (15 in total), as follows:

**Base ring:** Using Yarn A, 12 ch, join with sl st.
**Round 1:** 1 ch, 18 dc into ring, sl st to 1st dc (18 sts).
**Round 2:** 1 ch, into same st as 1 ch, * 1 dc, 3 ch, miss 2 sts, repeat from * 6 times, sl st to 1st dc.
**Round 3:** 1 ch, work a petal of (1 dc, 3 ch, 5 tr, 3 ch, 1 dc) into each of 6 x 3-ch arches, sl st to 1st dc.
**Round 4:** 1 ch, (1 dc between 2 dc on round 3, 5 ch behind petal of 3rd round) 6 times, sl st to 1st dc.
**Round 5:** 1 ch, work a petal of (1 dc, 3 ch, 7 tr, 3 ch, 1 dc) into each of next 6 x 5-ch arches, sl st to 1st dc.
Fasten off.

**Round 6:** Using Yarn B join between 2 dc, 1 ch, (1 dc between 2 dc on round 5, 6 ch behind petal of 5th round) 6 times, sl st to 1st dc.
**Round 7:** Sl st into next ch, 3 ch (count as 1 tr), * (4 tr, 2 ch, 1 tr) all into same arch, 6 tr into next arch, (2 tr, 2 ch, 4 tr) all into next arch ** 1 tr into next arch, rep from * to **, sl st to top of 3 ch.
**Round 8:** 3 ch (count as 1 tr), 1 tr into each tr all round with (3 tr, 2 ch, 3 tr) into each 2-ch corner sp, ending sl st to top of 3 ch.
Fasten off.

**Round 9:** Using Yarn C join into same place, 1 ch, 1 dc into same st as 1 ch, * 1 dc into next st, work a 3-ch picot of (3 ch, sl st down through top of last dc made) twice, 1 dc into each of next 3 sts, work (3-ch picot, 1 dc into next st) twice, (1 dc, 7 ch, 1 dc) into corner 2-ch sp, (1 dc into next st, 3-ch picot) twice, 1 dc into each of next 3 sts, (3-ch picot, 1 dc into next st) twice, 1 dc into next st, rep from * 3 times omitting dc at end of last rep, sl st to 1st dc.
**Round 10:** Sl st across to top of next 3-ch picot 1 ch, 1 dc into same picot, * 5 ch, miss next picot, 1 dc into next picot, 5 ch, (1 dc, 7 ch, 1 dc) into corner 7-ch arch (5 ch, miss next picot, 1 dc into next picot) twice, 5 ch, 1 dc into next picot; rep from * 3 times omitting dc at end of last rep, sl st to 1st dc.
Fasten off.

## FINISHING

Lightly press each square, referring to the ball band (see page 137).

Overcast each square together, alternating the two colourways to create a patchwork grid of 5 squares by 3 squares.

### Double-knot embroidery

With right side facing, work a double-knot embroidery stitch along each seam in Yarn D (see page 135).

### Edging

With right side facing, work 1 row of tr in Yarn C along the side edges of blanket, working into every alternate stitch.

Change to Yarn D, and work picot edge all around blanket: Working into loops from previous row, * 3 ch, 1 dc in 1st of these ch, miss 1 st, 1 dc in next st; rep from * to end. Fasten off.

Using Yarn B in your preferred colourway, make 4 pompoms of approximately 4.5cm (1¾in) diameter (see page 136) and sew one into each corner of the blanket.

The nostalgic appeal of this cute little cardigan is undeniable – from the soft mauve colour to the pretty shape and the flower-shaped buttons. Alicia Paulson dreams of a place in the Midwest where the summers seem impossibly long, where the beds are dressed in crisp white cotton, where a neighbour's porch swing rocks gently in the breeze and the lightning bugs hover. Making this perfect baby's cardigan gives you a little taste of that magical place.

# 'Maisie' Cardigan   Alicia Paulson

## MATERIALS
Five (five, six) 50g balls Debbie Bliss Baby Cashmerino, shade 608 Mauve
3mm crochet hook, or size hook needed to match tension
4mm crochet hook
3 buttons, approximately 1cm (½in) diameter
Tapestry needle

## MEASUREMENTS
**To fit age:** 3-6 months (6-12 months, 12-24 months).
**Finished chest circumference:** 45 (50, 55)cm/18 (20, 22)in.

## NOTE
Instructions for larger sizes are given in parentheses. Where there is only one figure, it applies to all sizes

## TENSION
20 sts and 15 rows = 10cm (4in) over yoke-pattern stitch, using 3mm crochet hook.

## ABBREVIATIONS
See page 120

## BACK YOKE
Using 3mm hook, ch 50 (54, 58).
**Row 1 (RS):** Htr in 3rd ch from hook and in each ch across to end; turn [48 (52, 56) sts].
**Row 2:** Ch 2, htr in each st across to end; turn.

### Armhole shaping
**Row 1:** Ch 2, htr2tog (dec made); pattern across to last 2 sts, htr2tog; turn [46 (50, 54) sts].
**Rows 2-5:** Repeat row 1. 38 (42, 46) sts after row 5.
**Row 6:** Ch 2, htr in each st across to end; turn.
Repeat row 6 until back measures approximately 10 (11.5, 13)cm/ 4 (4½, 5)in from beginning ending with a WS row. Fasten off.

## LEFT FRONT YOKE
Using 3mm hook, ch 26 (28, 30).
**Row 1 (RS):** Htr in 3rd ch from hook and in each ch across to end; turn [24 (26, 28) sts].
**Row 2:** Ch 2, htr in each st across to end; turn.

### Left front armhole shaping
**Row 1:** Ch 2, htr2tog (dec made); htr in each st across to end; turn [23 (25, 27) sts].
**Row 2:** Ch 2, htr in each st across to last 2 sts, htr2tog; turn [22 (24, 26) sts].
**Rows 3-5:** Repeat Rows 1 and 2. 19 (21, 23) sts after row 5.
**Row 6:** Ch 2, htr in each st across; turn.
Repeat row 6 until left front reaches approximately 6 (8, 9)cm/2½ (3, 3½)in from beginning ending with a WS row.

### Left front neck shaping

**Row 1 (RS):** Ch 2, htr in each st across, leaving last 8 (10, 10) sts unworked; turn [11 (11, 13) sts].
**Row 2:** Ch 2, htr2tog, htr in each st across to end; turn [10 (10, 12) sts].
**Row 3:** Ch 2, htr in each st across to last 2 sts, htr2tog; turn [9 (9, 11) sts].
**Row 4:** Ch 2, htr in each st across to end; turn.
Repeat row 4 until LF measures 10 (11.5, 13)cm/4 (4½, 5)in from beg. Fasten off.

### RIGHT FRONT YOKE

Make as for left front, reversing armhole and neck shaping.
**Note:** For neck shaping, on RS row sl st in 1st 8 (10, 10) sts then continue pattern across. Complete as for left front.

### SLEEVES

Using 3mm hook, ch 28 (30, 32).
**Row 1 (RS):** Htr in 3rd ch from hook, htr in next 10 (11, 12) ch, 2 htr in next 6 ch, htr in next 10 (11, 12) ch; turn [32 (34, 36) sts].
**Row 2:** Ch 2, 2 htr in 1st st, htr in each st across to last st, 2 htr in last st; turn [34 (36, 38) sts].
**Rows 3-5:** Repeat row 2 three times more; turn [40 (42, 44) sts].
**Row 6:** Ch 2, htr in each st across to end; turn.
Repeat row 6 until sleeve measures 8 (9.5, 11)cm/3¼ (3¾, 4¼)in.

### Sleeve edging

**Row 1:** Ch 2, htr in next st, (htr in next 5 sts, htr2tog in next st) 6 times, htr in last htr; turn [34 (36, 38) sts].
**Row 2:** Ch 2, miss 1st st, tr in next st, dc in previous st, (miss next st, tr in next st, dc in previous st) across to end; turn.
**Row 3:** Ch 1, dc in each st across to end. Fasten off.

### LOWER PART OF CARDIGAN

With wrong sides facing, stitch right front and left front to back piece at shoulders. Stitch sleeves into armholes, gather and ease around top if necessary. Stitch up sides and underarms.
With RS facing and using 4mm hook, join yarn at bottom edge of left front.

**Row 1:** Ch 1, working in bottom loops of foundation chain, (dc in next st, 2 dc in next st) across to end [144 (156, 168) sts].
**Row 2:** Ch 2, miss 1st st, tr in next st, dc in previous st. (Miss next st, tr in next st, dc in previous st) across to end; turn.
Repeat row 2 until bodice measures 24 (27, 29)cm/9½ (10½, 11½)in from shoulder, ending with a WS row; turn.
**Next Row:** Ch 1, dc in each st across to end. Fasten off.

### TRIM

With RS facing and using 3mm hook, join yarn with sl st at lower edge of right front yoke.
Ch 5 (or as many as necessary to go around button) to form loop for button, dc evenly halfway up yoke, ch 5 to form loop for button, dc evenly up to top of yoke, ch 5 to form loop for button, dc in same st twice to turn corner.
Dc evenly around neck edge and down front of yoke, making 3 dc in last st of right front to turn corner.
Fasten off.

### FINISHING

Weave in all ends and block lightly (see page 137).
Sew buttons to yoke approximately 3cm (1¼in) apart, directly opposite button loops.

Syd has been lovingly designed to appeal to children of all ages – even adult ones. The result is a toy that can be played with and loved by little ones, or sit on a chair or bed to keep more mature 'children' in touch with their childhood. Syd is slightly wonky and the handmade quality means that whoever crochets this rabbit will make him slightly differently and give him a unique character.

# 'Syd' Rabbit    Claire Montgomerie

## MATERIALS

Two 50g balls Blue Sky Alpacas Melange, shade 805 Huckleberry (Yarn A)

One 50g ball Blue Sky Alpacas Sportweight in each of the following shades: 30 Blue Sky (Yarn B), 517 Lemondrop (Yarn C), 506 Natural Streaky Brown, or any oddments of yarn for embroidering finishing touches (Yarn D)

4mm and 2.5mm crochet hooks

Toy stuffing

Tapestry needle

Small pompom maker or carboard to make template (see page 136)

## MEASUREMENTS

**Length (from top of head to feet):** 38cm (15in).

**Length (from top of head to bottom of body):** 27cm (10½in).

**Belly circumference (at widest):** 32cm (12½in).

**Span of arms (opened wide):** 38cm (15in).

## TENSION

Obtaining a certain tension is not essential, but when making toys, ensure that you crochet tightly; otherwise the stuffing will show through the gaps. This means you may have to use a hook that you would usually consider much too small for your yarn.

## ABBREVIATIONS

See page 120.

## SPECIAL ABBREVIATIONS

dec – decrease 1 by working 2 sts together.

## BODY

Begin stuffing body when you start to decrease for neck. It will be easier than stuffing when the body is finished.

Using 4mm hook and Yarn A, ch 3, 8 dc in 2nd ch from hook, join round with sl st.

**Round 1:** Ch 1, 1 dc into same st, * 2 dc in next st, rep from * to end, join round with sl st (16 sts).

**Round 2:** Ch 1, 2 dc in next st, * 1 dc in next st, 2 dc in next st, rep from * to end, join round with sl st (24 sts).

**Round 3:** Ch 1, 2 dc in next st, * 1 dc in next st, 2 dc in next st, rep from * to end, join round with sl st (36 sts).

**Round 4:** Ch 1, 1 dc in next st, 2 dc into next st, * 2 dc, 2 dc into next st, rep from * to end, join round with sl st (48 sts).

**Round 5:** Ch 1, 1 dc in each st all round (48 sts).

**Round 6:** Ch 1, 2 dc, 2 dc into next st, * 3 dc, 2 dc into next st, rep from * to end, join round with sl st (60 sts).

**Round 7:** Ch 1, work 1 dc in each st all round (60 sts).

**Round 8:** Ch 1, 3 dc, 2 dc into next st, * 4 dc, 2 dc into next st, rep from * to end, join round with sl st (72 sts).

**Round 9:** Sl st all around, working through back loop of each st only (72 sts).

Work 3 rounds straight in dc (72 sts).

**Round 13:** Ch 1, 4 dc, 2 dc into next st, * 5 dc, 2 dc into next st, rep from * to end, join round with sl st (84 sts).

Work 4 rounds straight in dc (84 sts).

**Round 18:** Ch 1, 4 dc, dec 1 st, * 5 dc, dec 1 st, rep from * to end, join round with sl st (72 sts).

Work 4 rounds straight in dc (72 sts).

**Round 23:** Ch 1, 3 dc, dec 1 st, * 4 dc, dec 1 st, rep from * to end, join round with sl st (60 sts).

Work 6 rounds straight in dc (60 sts).

**Round 30:** Ch 1, 2 dc, dec 1 st, * 3 dc, dec 1 st, rep from * to end, join round with sl st (48 sts).

Work 4 rounds straight in dc (48 sts).

**Round 35:** Ch 1, 1 dc, dec 1 st, * 2 dc, dec 1 st, rep from * to end, join round with sl st (36 sts).

Work straight for 6 rows in dc (36 sts).

**Round 42:** Dec all around row (18 sts).

Work 1 round straight in dc.

**Round 44:** Dec all around round (9 sts).

Fasten off yarn.

## HEAD

Using 4mm hook and Yarn A, ch 3, 6 dc in 2nd ch from hook, join round with sl st.

**Round 1:** Ch 1, 1 dc into same st, * 2 dc in next st, rep from * to end, join round with sl st (12 sts).

**Round 2:** Ch 1, 2 dc in next st, * 1 dc in next st, 2 dc in next st, rep from * to end, join round with sl st (18 sts).

**Round 3:** Ch 1, 3 dc in next st, * 1 dc in next st, 3 dc in next st, rep from * to end, join round with sl st (24 sts).

Work 1 round straight in dc (24 sts).

**Round 5:** Ch 1, 2 dc, 2 dc into next st, * 3 dc, 2 dc into next st, rep from * to end, join round with sl st (30 sts).

Work 1 round straight in dc (30 sts).

**Round 7:** Ch 1, 3 dc, 2 dc into next st, * 4 dc, 2 dc into next st, rep from * to end, join round with sl st (36 sts).

Work 1 round straight in dc (36 sts).

**Round 9:** Ch 1, 4 dc, 2 dc into next st, * 5 dc, 2 dc into next st, rep from * to end, join round with sl st (42 sts).

Work 4 rounds straight in dc (42 sts).

**Round 14:** Ch 1, 4 dc, dec 1 st, * 5 dc, dec 1 st, rep from * to end, join round with sl st (36 sts).

Work 1 round straight in dc (36 sts).

**Round 16:** Ch 1, 3 dc, dec 1 st, * 4 dc, dec 1 st, rep from * to end, join round with sl st (30 sts).

Work 1 round straight in dc (30 sts).

**Round 18:** Ch 1, 2 dc, dec 1 st, * 3 dc, dec 1 st, rep from * to end, join round with sl st (24 sts).

**Round 19:** Ch 1, 1 dc, dec 1 st, * 2 dc, dec 1 st, rep from * to end, join round with sl st (18 sts).

Fasten off yarn.

Stuff head with toy filling and sew to top of body, ensuring that each part is filled sufficiently so that the head does not flop over.

## ARMS

Using 4mm hook and Yarn A, ch 3, 5 dc in 2nd ch from hook, join round with sl st.

**Round 1:** Ch 1, 1 dc into same st, * 2 dc in next st, rep from * to end, join round with sl st (10 sts).

**Round 2:** Ch 1, 2 dc in next st, * 1 dc in next st, 2 dc in next st, rep from * to end, join round with sl st (15 sts).

**Round 3:** Work round in dc.

Work as round 3 until arm measures approximately 16cm (6½in), beginning stuffing halfway through, as this will be easier than stuffing at the end.

Fasten off yarn.

Make one more arm in the same way and sew each to body.

## LEGS

Using 4mm hook and Yarn A, ch 3, 5 dc in 2nd ch from hook, join round with sl st.

**Round 1:** Ch 1, 1 dc into same st, * 2 dc in next st, rep from * to end, join round with sl st (10 sts).

**Round 2:** Work round in dc.

Work as round 2 until leg measures approx 6cm (2½in).

Fasten off yarn.

Make one more leg in the same way.

## FEET

Using 4mm hook and Yarn A, ch 3, 6 dc in 2nd ch from hook, join round with sl st.

**Round 1:** Ch 1, 1 dc into same st, * 2 dc in next st, rep from * to end, join round with sl st (12 sts).

**Round 2:** Ch 1, dc in 1st dc, htr in each of next 2 dc, 3 tr in next dc, htr in each of next 2 dc, dc in next dc, htr in each of next 2 dc, 3 tr in next dc, dc to end of round, sl st to join round (16 sts).

**Round 3:** Ch 1, dc to centre st of 3-tr inc of previous round, 4 dc, 1 htr, 2 tr into next st, 3 tr into next st, 2 tr into next st, 1 htr, dc to end of round, join round with sl st (20 sts).

**Round 4:** Ch 1, dc to centre st of 3-dc inc of previous round, 3 dc into next st, dc to 1 st before htr of previous round, htr into dc, tr into htr, 2 tr into next tr, 2 trtr into tr, 2 tr into next st, 3 tr into central st, 2 tr into next st, 2 trtr into next st, 2 tr into next st, tr, htr, dc to end of round, sl st to join round (30 sts).

**Round 5:** Ch 1, dc to centre inc st of previous round, 3 dc into next st, dc to 1st htr of previous round, htr, tr, 2 tr into next st, 2 tr into next st, 2 trtr into next st, tr into each st across, to 2nd trtr of previous round, 2 trtr into next st, 2 tr into next st, 2 tr into next st, tr, htr, dc to end of round, join with sl st (38 sts).

Fasten off yarn.

Make 1 more foot piece in Yarn A and one each of Yarn B and Yarn C.

Sew one Yarn A and one Yarn C foot piece together and stuff. Repeat with remaining two foot pieces in Yarn A and Yarn B. With Yarn A side on top and the other colour for the sole, sew a foot to each leg and stuff the legs. Sew each leg to body.

Sew tummy into place on body. Add a row of blanket stitch around the edge if desired (see page 134).

## EARS

### Left ear

Using 4mm hook and Yarn A, ch 19.

**Row 1:** Work 1 htr into 3rd ch from hook, work 1 tr into each ch to end, working only through one loop, in end ch work 3 tr, and cont along other side of chain, working 1 tr in each ch to end, working through rem loop of each ch. Ch 3, turn (39 sts).

**Row 2:** Work as for row 1, but working through both loops of each st.

**Row 3:** Work in tr to 3 sts from end st, work 1 htr into next st, tr, 3 trtr into end st, tr, htr, tr to end of round.

Fasten off yarn.

Work one more ear piece in Yarn B. Sew two ear pieces together, fold in half and sew together along bottom. Attach to head.

### Right ear

Using 4mm hook and Yarn A, ch 23.

**Row 1:** Work 1 htr into 3rd ch from hook, work 1 tr into each ch to end, working only through one loop, in end ch work 3 tr, and cont along other side of chain, working 1 tr in each ch to end, working through rem loop of each ch. Ch 3, turn (39 sts).

**Rows 2 and 3:** Work 2 more rows in this way, but working through both loops of each st.

Fasten off yarn.

Work one more ear piece in Yarn C. Sew two ear pieces together, fold in half and sew together along bottom. Attach to head.

## FINISHING

Embroider face and extra embellishments as required in Yarn D or oddments of yarn.

Make two eyes using 2.5mm hook and Yarn B as follows:
Ch 3, 4 dc in 2nd ch from hook, join round with sl st.

**Round 1:** Ch 1, dc into same st, 2 dc into each st around (8 sts).
Fasten off yarn.

If you wish, you can make the next eye bigger by adding one more round in the same way as round 1.

Sew eyes to head.

For the tail, make a pompom of approximately 4.5cm (1¾in) in diameter (see page 136), using one or an assortment of the yarns. Sew the tail in place at the bottom rear of the body.

## TUMMY

Using 4mm hook and Yarn C, ch 3, 6 dc in 2nd ch from hook, join round with sl st.

**Round 1:** Ch 1, 1 dc into same st, * 2 dc in next st, rep from * to end, join round with sl st (12 sts).

**Round 2:** Ch 1, 2 dc in next st, * 1 dc in next st, 2 dc in next st, rep from * to end, join round with sl st (18 sts).

**Round 3:** Ch 1, 3 dc in next st, * 1 dc in next st, 3 dc in next st, rep from * to end, join round with sl st (24 sts).

**Round 4:** Ch 1, 2 dc, 2 dc into next st, * 3 dc, 2 dc into next st, rep from * to end, join round with sl st (30 sts).

**Round 5:** Ch 1, 3 dc, 2 dc into next st, * 4 dc, 2 dc into next st, rep from * to end, join round with sl st (36 sts).

**Round 6:** Ch 3, 4 tr, 2 tr into next st, * 5 tr, 2 tr into next st, rep from * to end, join round with sl st (42 sts).

**Round 7:** Ch 3, 5 tr, 2 tr into next st, * 6 tr, 2 tr into next st, rep from * to end, join round with sl st (48 sts).

**Round 8:** Ch 3, 6 tr, 2 tr into next st, * 7 tr, 2 tr into next st, rep from * to end, join round with sl st (54 sts).
Fasten off yarn.

This traditional 'clasp' purse adds a touch of elegance to any outfit and is just the right size to hold money, compact and lipstick – making it ideal for parties or weddings. The berry coloured yarn is offset by the vintage floral lining.

# Butterfly-Stitch Purse  Kate Samphier

## MATERIALS

One 50g ball ggh Bel Air, shade 3 Deep Plum
5mm crochet hook
30cm (¼yd) fabric for lining backing (bottle-green baby cord)
30cm (¼yd) fabric for inner lining (floral linen)
One medium-sized silver purse frame
Sewing needle and thread
Fabric glue

## MEASUREMENTS

Approximately 10 x 16cm (4 x 6½in).

## TENSION

1 motif = approximately 3.5cm (1½in).
Obtaining a certain tension is not essential.

## ABBREVIATIONS

See page 120.

## PURSE

Make 2 purse panels, as follows.
Using 5mm hook make a chain of 31 sts.
**Row 1:** 3 ch, then work in tr to end of row.
**Row 2:** 3 ch, 1 tr in 2nd tr, * miss 2 sts, 3 tr in next st, miss 2 sts, (1 tr, 3 ch, 1 tr) in next st *, repeat from * 3 times, miss 2 sts, 2 tr in last st.
**Row 3:** Ch, 2 tr in 3-ch space of previous row, * 1 dc in 2nd of 3 tr of previous row, 7 tr in next 3-ch space *, repeat from * and finish with 3 tr in last 3-ch space instead of 7 tr.
**Row 4:** 3 ch, 1 tr in 1st tr, * 3 tr in dc of previous row, (1 tr, 3 ch, 1 tr) in 4th tr of group of 7 tr *.
**Row 5:** Repeat row 3.
**Row 6:** Repeat row 4.

### Decrease

**Row 7:** Dc into 3rd tr, * 7 tr in 3-ch space, 1 dc in 2nd of 3 tr of previous row, * dc.
**Row 8:** 3 ch, * 1 tr, 3 ch, 1 tr in 4th of previous 7 tr, 3 tr into dc, * dc in 4th st of previous 7.
**Row 9:** Dc into 3 tr, * 7 tr in 3-ch space, 1 dc in 2nd of 3 tr of previous row, * miss 1 st, dc.
**Row 10:** 3 ch, (1 tr, 3 ch, 1 tr) into 4th of 7 tr, 3 tr of dc, (1 tr, 3 tr, 1 tr), into 4th of 7 tr, 3 ch, miss 3 st dc. Fasten off.

## ASSEMBLY AND FINISHING

**1.** Using the purse frame and the completed crochet panel, draw a template from which to cut the linings, allowing at least 1cm (½in) all round for seams and extra fabric at the hinge point to allow the purse to open. Cut 2 pieces of lining material and two pieces of backing material.
**2.** Tack backing fabric to wrong side of crochet panels.
**3.** Using a needle and thread, sew crochet panels to backing fabric.
**4.** With crochet sides facing each other, sew seams together from hinge point, down side, across bottom and up to other hinge point. Turn crochet side out.
**5.** With right sides together, sew bottom parts of inner lining fabric from hinge point, down side, across bottom and up to other hinge point. Finish raw edge with zigzag stitch or make a French seam (see page 91).
**6.** Place lining in crochet bag. Turn the edges in, adjusting the top of lining to fit purse.
**7.** On each side of purse, slipstitch top part of lining, with raw edges turned under, to top part of crochet, beginning where stitching stops at the hinge. Press if necessary.
**8.** Following manufacturer's instructions, apply glue generously to one side of purse frame and to top and side edges of fabric around one side of purse opening. Allow glue to dry for 5 minutes, or as recommended.
**9.** Insert one side of purse into frame, starting at the hinge and working around the top and down the other side. Check that the lining is also inserted evenly. Allow to dry for 15 minutes, then glue the other side of the purse fabric into the frame in the same way.

Show your favourite furry friend how much you love him by crocheting this cosy sweater-coat for him. It'll keep him toasty on snowy winter days or brisk early morning walks, but it's comfy to wear so it won't stop him having fun chasing sticks, balls, other dogs – or his own tail. The 'hoodie' design, complete with jaunty pompom, means he won't loose his street-cred, either; he'll still be the smartest dog on the block – and in the park.

# 'Woody' Dog Coat

## Bee Clinch

### MATERIALS
Three 50g balls Lana Grossa Royal Tweed, shade 36 Pink (Yarn A)
One 50g ball Rowan Cashsoft (DK), shade 509 Lime (Yarn B)
5mm crochet hook
Tapestry needle
4 vintage buttons, approximately 2cm (¾in) diameter
Small pompom maker or stiff cardboard to make pompom
    template (see page 136)

### MEASUREMENTS
To fit a small dog, such as a terrier, poodle or small spaniel.
**Length:** From shoulder seam to bottom edge of back, approximately 30cm (12in).
**Hood:** From tip of hood to shoulder seam, approximately 18cm (7in).
**Chest circumference:** Approximately 47cm (18½in).

### TENSION
12 st to 10cm (4in).

### ABBREVIATIONS
See page 120.

### SPECIAL ABBREVIATIONS
**ps – puff stitch:** To make a puff stitch of 4 half treble stitches, wrap yarn round hook, insert hook into stitch, wrap yarn again and draw a loop through (3 loops on hook). Repeat this step three times more, inserting the hook into the same stitch each time (9 loops on hook), wrap yarn and draw through all loops on hook. (See also page 123, where this stitch is shown worked in an openwork fabric.)

## NOTE

This coat, with the cute pompom hood, has been specially designed for a pampered little dog, Woody. Small dogs normally feel the cold more than bigger dogs, unless it's exceptionally cold. But even then, a larger dog might look better in a simpler sweater, without a hood!

## BACK

Using Yarn A ch 37 + 2. Turn.

**Row 1:** Dc into 2nd ch from hook, (1 dc, 1 ch, miss next stitch for buttonhole) continue in dc to end, ch 1, turn.

**Row 2:** Dc into 1st stitch, ps into ch sp, dc, * ps, dc; repeat from *, ch 1, turn.

**Row 3:** Repeat row 1, omitting buttonhole.

Every alt row will follow this pattern.

**Row 4:** Dc into 1st stitch, * dc, ps, dc, repeat from * to last stitch, dc, ch 1, turn.

**Row 6:** 1 dc, * ps, 1 dc, repeat from * 3 times, dc to last 6 stitches, repeat from * to end, ch 1, turn.

**Row 8:** 1 dc, * dc, ps, repeat from * 3 times, dc to last 7 stitches, repeat from * to last stitch, dc, ch 1, turn.

Repeat this last 4-row pattern until the work measures 10cm (4in) finishing with an 8th row.

Repeat row 1, including buttonhole.

**Next row:** As for row 6, but 1st ps will be in the 1st ch sp.

Continue in pattern until work measures 19cm (7½in).

### Shaping

**Row 1:** Sl st 1, ch 1, dc to end, ch 1, turn.

**Row 2:** Sl st 1, ch 2, * (ps, dc) repeat 4 times, dc to last 8 sts, repeat from * to end, ch 1, turn.

Repeat rows 1 and 2 four more times (10 rows in total). Finish with 2nd shaping row.

**Final row:** Dc, ch 1, miss st, (buttonhole), dc to end. Fasten off.

## FRONT

Ch 14 + 1.

**Next and continuing rows:** Dc into 2nd ch from hook dc to end. Ch 1, turn.

Continue until work measures 19cm (7½in).

**Next row:** Sl st 1, ch 1, dc to end.

Repeat this row 12 times in total. Fasten off.

## HOOD

Ch 30 + 1.

**Row 1:** Dc in 2nd ch from hook, dc to end, ch 1, turn.

**Row 2:** Dc 1, * ps, dc, repeat from * to end, ch 1, turn.

Repeat row 1, omitting buttonhole (12 rows in total). Fasten off.

## FINISHING

With wrong sides together, dc along long side of back (without buttonholes) and front pieces to join.

Join firmly at neck opposite buttonhole.

Sew buttons on front piece to match buttonholes on left side of front.

With wrong sides together, fold hood in half along long edge and dc along one side.

Match centre seam of hood to centre of back and pin.

Join hood and body with dc.

Using Yarn B, make a pompom of approximately 4.5cm (1¾in) diameter (see page 136) and sew onto top point of hood.

Now, walk the dawg!

Far too pretty to hide away in a wardrobe, this lovely padded hanger would make a great gift for everyone from your grandma to your teenage sister. Covered in the softest fluffy yarn, it will be far kinder to delicate dresses or knits than a standard hanger, and will look so much more stylish. To make it even more special, embellish it with ribbon, beads, sequins or buttons, then use it to display a favourite dress.

# Hanger with Flower  Bee Clinch

## MATERIALS

One 50g ball ggh Amelie, shade 12 Soft Blue (Yarn A)
One 50g ball Jaeger Siena 4-Ply Cotton in each of the following
    shades: 404 Lavender (Yarn B), 405 Seaspray (Yarn C)
3mm and 6mm crochet hooks
32cm (12½in) padded hanger (alternatively, use a wooden or plastic
    hanger and cover it with wadding yourself)
5 small vintage buttons, approximately 1cm (½in) diameter
Tapestry needle
Small amount of glue

## MEASUREMENTS

**Length of hanger:** 32cm (12½in).
**Diameter of flowers:** Approximately 5cm (2in).

## TENSION

12 st over 10cm (4in), using a 6mm crochet hook.

## ABBREVIATIONS

See page 120.

## NOTES

If your hanger is a different length, use tension guide to estimate
how many chain to make.

## HANGER COVER

With 6mm hook and Yarn A, ch 40 + 1 (for hanger measuring
32cm/12½in).
**Row 1:** Dc into 2nd ch from hook, dc to end, ch 1, turn.
**Row 2:** Dc into 1st stitch, dc to end.
Repeat row 1 until 7 rows completed. Fasten off.

## FLOWER CASCADE

With 3mm hook and Yarn B, ch 4. Sl st into 1st ch to form circle.
**Round 1:** * Ch 4, into circle make 3 trtr (yarn round hook 3 times), 4 ch,
sl st into circle. * Repeat from * to * 4 more times (5 petals in total).
Ch 40 after last sl st, ch 4, sl st into 4th ch from hook to form circle.
Repeat from * to * 5 times to create another 5-petal flower.
After last sl st, continue to sl st along 40-ch length to first flower.
Sl st into back of flower. Fasten off.
Make another cascade set, as above, using Yarn C.
Make one flower using Yarn B omitting sl-st cord.

## FINISHING

Using a tapestry needle, sew in all yarn ends.
Fold hanger cover in half, with wrong sides together, and close seams
with dc, leaving a 12cm (4¾in) opening at the top. Insert hanger and
close opening using tapestry needle and yarn.
Gently press flowers (referring to ball bands).
Using Yarn B or Yarn C as appropriate, sew buttons to the centre
of each flower.
Work metal hook of hanger through the slip-stitch cord between
flowers, adjusting lengths as preferred.
Bind a long length of Yarn C around metal hook, pushing down flower
cords close to base. Finish binding at tip of hook and dab a small
amount of glue to attach.
Glue the single Yarn B flower to the base of the hook.

Add instant panache to any item in your wardrobe with this gorgeous peony corsage – a simple way to embellish clothes and give them a fresh new look. Whether you use it to dress up a cardigan, jacket or coat lapel, or pin it onto a bag, this blowsy bloom will give the garment a pretty, feminine touch.

# Peony Corsage  Kate Jenkins

## MATERIALS
One 50g ball ggh Bel Air in each of the following shades:
 1 Pink (Yarn A), 2 Lilac (Yarn B), 3 Deep Plum (Yarn C),
 20 Dark Olive (Yarn D), 21 Pale Olive (Yarn E)
4.5mm crochet hook
Wadding or scraps of yarn to stuff bobble
Tapestry needle

## MEASUREMENTS
**Central bobble:** Approximately 5cm (2in) diameter.
**Inner petals:** Approximately 12cm (4¾in) diameter.
**Outer petals:** Approximately 14cm (5½in) diameter.
**Leaves:** 5cm (2in) long; 5cm (2in) at widest point.

## TENSION
Obtaining a certain tension is not essential; however, it should be fairly tight - especially for the bobble, so the stuffing does not show through.

## ABBREVIATIONS
See page 120.

## NOTE
If you wish to add more colour detail to the petals when completed, work around the edges in picot crochet (3 ch, 1 sl st) using an additional contrasting colour.

## BOBBLE
Using Yarn A, 6 ch sl st into 1st chain to form circle.
**Round 1:** 3 ch, 20 tr, sl st into top of 3 ch.
**Round 2:** 3 ch ,1 tr into each tr of previous round, sl st into top of 3 ch.
**Round 3:** Repeat round 2.
**Round 4:** 3 ch, work 2trtog (repeat 10 times), sl st into top of 3 ch.
At this stage, start to fill bobble with stuffing (wadding or yarn scraps).
**Round 5:** * 2 ch, work 2dctog, repeat from * 5 times.

Fasten off and sew in ends.

## INNER PETALS (Make 5 in Yarn A and 5 in Yarn B)
**Row 1:** 5 ch, miss 1 ch, 1 tr into next 4 ch, 1 ch, turn.
**Row 2:** 2 tr into 1st tr, 1 tr into each of next 3 tr, 2 tr into last tr, 1 ch, turn.
**Row 3:** 2 tr into 1st tr, 1 tr into next 4 tr, 2 tr into last tr, 1 ch, turn.
**Row 4:** 2 tr into 1st tr, 1 tr into next 6 tr, 2 tr into last tr, 1 ch, turn.
**Row 5:** Work 3trtog, 1 tr into next 4 tr, work 3trtog.
Fasten off and sew in ends.

## OUTER PETALS (Make 5 in Yarn C)
**Row 1:** Work 7 ch, miss 1 ch, 1 tr into next 6 ch, 1 ch, turn.
**Row 2:** 2 tr into next tr, 1 tr into next 4 tr, 2 tr into last tr, 1 ch, turn.
**Row 3:** 2 tr into 1st tr, 1 tr into next 6 tr, 2 tr into last tr, 1 ch, turn.
**Row 4:** 2 tr into next tr, 1 tr into next 8 tr, 2 tr into last tr, 1 ch, turn.
**Row 5:** 2 tr into next tr, 1 tr into next 10 tr, 2 tr into last tr, 1 ch, turn.
**Row 6:** Work 3trtog, 1 tr into next 8 tr, work 3trtog.
Fasten off and sew in ends.
When all petals are complete sew onto bobble, starting with inner petals.

## LEAF (Make 2 in Yarn D)
**Row 1:** 4 ch, miss 1 ch, 3 tr into next 3 ch, 1 ch, turn.
**Row 2:** 2 tr into 1st tr, 1 tr, 2 tr into last tr, 1 ch, turn.
**Row 3:** 2 tr into 1st tr, 1 tr into next 3 tr, 2 tr into last tr, 1 ch, turn.
**Row 4:** 2 tr into 1st tr, 1 tr into next 5 tr, 2 tr into last tr, 1 ch, turn.
**Row 5:** 2 tr into 1st tr, 1 tr into next 7 tr, 2 tr into last tr, 1 ch, turn.
**Row 6:** Work 2trtog, 1 tr into next 7 tr, work 2trtog, 1 ch, turn.
**Row 7:** Work 2trtog, 1 tr into next 5 tr, work 2trtog, 1 ch, turn.
**Row 8:** Work 2trtog, 1 tr into next 5 tr, work 2trtog, 1 ch, turn.
**Row 9:** Work 2trtog, 1 tr into next 3 tr, work 2trtog, 1 ch, turn.
**Row 10:** Work 3trtog, and fasten off.
Change to Yarn E and join to bottom of leaf; work 2 rounds of tr into edge of leaf. Fasten off and sew in ends.
Using a tapestry needle and Yarn E, embroider details vein on leaves.

Gorgeous and textural, the wonderful chunky raised bobble stitch in off-white yarn makes this the perfect summer handbag to complement any outfit, from a jeans-and-T combo to a fifties floral prom dress. Designed in a classic purse shape with chunky wooden handles, this elegant bag is roomy enough for all your everyday essentials but not so outsize as to be cumbersome. You could always use it for your crochet, knitting or sewing kit, too. Cut up a favourite old summer dress to make a colourful and pretty lining.

# Bobble-Stitch Handbag

## Kate Jenkins

### MATERIALS
Ten 50g balls ggh Big Easy, shade 001 White
5mm crochet hook
2 pieces of lining material, 54 x 34cm (21 x 13½in)
Matching sewing thread
Sewing needle
Sewing machine
Wooden bag handles, 32cm (12½in) wide

### MEASUREMENTS
30cm (12in) deep, excluding handles.
48cm (19in) wide at base.

### TENSION
14 sts per 10cm (4in). One complete pattern repeat (bobble plus shell) = approximately 5cm (2in), using size 5mm crochet hook, or the size to obtain the correct tension.

### ABBREVIATIONS
See page 120.

### SPECIAL ABBREVIATIONS
**BRtr – back raised treble:** Yarn round hook and insert hook from back to front and right to left over stem of next stitch in row below, complete treble.

## BAG

Make 61 ch.

**Row 1:** Miss 1 ch, work 1 tr into each ch to end, 1 ch, turn.

**Rows 2-3:** Repeat row 1.

**Row 4:** ** 1 tr, miss 2 tr, then work 1 BRtr behind the next tr of previous row, work 1 BRtr behind next tr, then work 1 BRtr behind first and then second of the previous 2 tr missed at the beginning. 1 tr then 8 dtr into next tr leaving last loop of each st on hook, draw through all 8 loops (bobble made), 1 ch, 1 tr into next tr, repeat from ** to end.

**Rows 5-25:** Repeat row 4 twenty-one times.

**Row 26:** 1 tr in each st, 1 ch, turn.

**Rows 27-28:** Repeat row 26 twice.

Fasten off.

## LINING

**1.** Sew 1cm (½in) hems along both short sides of each piece.

**2.** Tack or pin pleats along top and bottom edges of lining to fit crochet bag measurements (see picture opposite).

**3.** With right sides facing and with a 1cm (½in) seam allowance, sew bottom edges of lining together using the sewing machine. Finish the raw edges with zigzag stitch or make a French seam to enclose raw edges (see page 91).

**4.** Sew up sides from bottom of bag, stopping 20cm (8in) from the top to allow for opening.

**5.** Place lining in crochet bag, with wrong sides together, and pin sides to opening edges.

**6.** Turn top edges of lining to wrong side to hide raw edges, adjust to fit, and pin in place; neatly slipstitch top edges of lining and bag together.

**7.** Pull top of crochet bag through the slots of the handles, and stitch neatly and securely to inside of bag.

**8.** Close side seams with slipstitch.

**9.** Close side seams with a double crochet seam. Work 1 row of bobbles (same as bobble used in bag) to both side seams.

# Techniques

## STANDARD ABBREVIATIONS

brtr – back raised treble
ch – chain
ch sp – chain space
cl – cluster
cont – continue
ctr – crossed treble
dc – double crochet
dec – decrease
dtr – double treble
frdc – front raised double crochet
frdtr – front raised double treble
frt – front
frtr – front raised treble
htr – half treble
inc – increase
lp(s) – loop(s)
ls – loop stitch
lps – loop puff stitch
p – picot
pc – popcorn
pf – puff stitch
qtr – quadruple treble
rem – remaining
rep – repeat
rev dc – reverse double crochet
rf – relief stitch
rnd(s) – round(s)
RS – right side
rdc – reverse double crochet (= rev dc)
s – spike
sk – Solomon's knot
sl st – slip stitch
sp(s) – space(s)
st(s) – stitch(es)
tch – turning chain
tog – together
tr – treble
ttr – triple treble
WS – wrong side
yrh – yarn round hook

# WORKING THE BASIC STITCHES

The patterns in this book assume a basic knowledge of crochet. Absolute beginners should consult a book with a detailed, illustrated introduction to the craft. Here, we give a brief rundown of the basic techniques, followed by the special techniques used for the patterns.

## HOLDING THE HOOK AND YARN

There are basically two ways of holding a crochet hook. You can hold it like a knife, with the shaft lying under your palm, or like a pencil, with the shaft lying between your thumb and index finger. In either case, the flat part of the shaft is grasped by the thumb and index finger and the hook itself (when at rest) is facing you.

There are several different ways of holding the yarn. One good way is to take it under, then completely around the little finger, then over the remaining fingers. The thumb and index finger hold the work and the raised middle finger tensions the yarn.

Beginners tend to work too tightly; if you do this, try to relax.

NOTE For left-handed readers: the words 'left' and 'right' have been avoided where possible in this section. Where they are used and where a right-handed method of working is shown in the illustrations, you will need to reverse the instructions and images.

## WORKING A CHAIN (abbreviation 'ch')

Virtually all crochet begins with a slip knot followed by a number of chain stitches, formed by inserting the hook through the slip knot, drawing a loop through and continuing to draw loops through until the required number of chain stitches have been worked.

If you look at the chain you will see that it has two distinct sides: one side - considered the front - is flat; the other has a 'bump', formed by the strand leading up to the next link. Normally the hook is inserted under either one or both sides of the front of the chain. Very occasionally you will be told to insert the hook through the 'bump' at the back of the work.

NOTE If you need to work a long chain, it is a good idea to leave a fairly long tail (30-40cm/12-16in) on the slip knot. If you find, when working the first row, that you've miscounted and are short of chain, you can work some more using this tail. If you have too many, you can unpick them.

## OTHER BASIC STITCHES

When working into fabric stitches, as opposed to chain stitches, the hook is normally inserted under both strands of the top of the stitch. At the end of a row, you will need to work one or more chain (called turning chain) to serve as the first stitch of the next row, the number depending on the height of the stitches to be worked in that row.

### Slip stitch (abbreviation 'sl st')

Insert the hook into the next stitch, draw a loop through both the stitch and the loop on the hook.

This stitch has virtually no height and is used mainly for joining parts of a fabric.

### Double crochet (abbreviation 'dc')

Insert the hook in the next stitch (or as instructed). Yarn round the hook and draw through loop (2 loops on hook). Yarn round hook and draw through both loops.

Number of turning chain: 1.

### Half-treble crochet (abbreviation 'htr')

Yarn round the hook, then insert the hook in the next stitch (or as instructed). Yarn round hook and draw a through loop (3 loops on hook). Yarn round hook and draw through all 3 loops.

Number of turning chain: 2.

### Treble (abbreviation 'tr')

Yarn round the hook and insert hook in the next stitch (or as instructed). Yarn round the hook and draw through loop (3 loops on hook). Yarn round the hook and draw through 2 loops (2 loops on hook). Yarn round the hook and draw through 2 loops.

Number of turning chain: 3

## KEEPING EDGES STRAIGHT

A common problem for beginners in crochet is managing to keep the edges straight. When starting a new row, make sure you work into the penultimate stitch of the previous row - not into the last one, from which the turning chain emerges. Also remember to work the last stitch of the new row into the turning chain of the previous row.

## TENSION

Whether you crochet loosely or tightly or somewhere in between, it's usually essential to obtain the tension specified in the pattern - that is, the same number of stitches and rows over a given measurement. A little variation won't matter in the case of a throw or a scarf, but if you're making a fitted garment, working to the wrong tension could result in a big disappointment: a baggy, shapeless garment or one that's too tight for comfort.

So, before you begin the project, make a swatch to check your tension. It will be time well spent.

### Making a tension swatch

1   Find out from the pattern the number of stitches and rows to 10cm/4in over the stitch pattern.

2   Using a crochet hook of the size recommended for obtaining the correct tension, make a length of chain adequate to make a swatch 15-20cm/6-8in wide in the stitch pattern.

3   Work enough rows to make the swatch 15-20cm/6-8in deep. Fasten off.

4   Block the swatch (see page 137).

5   Pin the swatch to a towel or flat pad, without stretching.

6   Place a pin between two stitches, a short distance from one edge. Then place a ruler or tape measure along that row, and insert another pin 10cm/4in away from the first pin.

7   Count the number of stitches between the pins.

8   Place a pin between two rows, a short way in from the bottom or top edge. Then place a ruler vertically over the rows, and insert another pin 10cm/4in away from the first pin.

9   Count the number of rows between these pins.

10  Compare your number of stitches and rows with the numbers given in the pattern's tension measurement. If you have more than the number stated, your crochet is too tight. Make another swatch using a larger hook.

11  If you have fewer rows/stitches than required, your crochet is too loose. Make another swatch using a smaller hook.

## CROCHET HOOK CONVERSIONS

In an ideal world we would all be using the same measurements. However, for those with old-fashioned or American hooks can convert them with this chart. If in doubt stick to the metric sizes as these are more accurate.

| METRIC | US |
| --- | --- |
| 2.25mm | B-1 |
| 2.75mm | C-2 |
| 3.25mm | D-3 |
| 3.5mm | E-4 |
| 3.75mm | F-5 |
| 4mm | G-6 |
| 4.5mm | 7 |
| 5mm | H-8 |
| 5.5mm | I-9 |
| 6mm | J-10 |
| 7mm | K-10½ |
| 8mm | L-11 |
| 9mm | M/N-13 |
| 10mm | N/P-15 |
| 15mm | P/Q |
| 16mm | Q |
| 19mm | S |

# SPECIAL STITCHES

## LOOPED PUFF STITCH (lps)

This stitch produces a softly textured effect, suitable for embellishing an openwork fabric. Stitches are worked into the chain space below.

1    * Wrap the yarn round the hook and insert the hook into the chain space below (fig. A).

2    Wrap the yarn round the hook again and pull a loop through, lifting it up to the required height (3 loops on hook) (fig. B).

3    Repeat from * 3 times (9 loops on hook) (fig. C).

4    Yarn round hook and draw the loop through all 9 loops. Yarn round hook and draw a loop through the loop on the hook to complete the puff stitch (fig. D). The sample shows four completed puff stitches (fig. E).

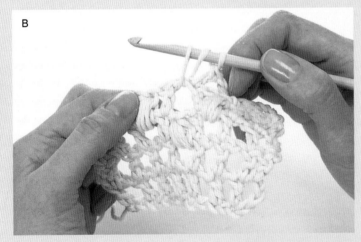

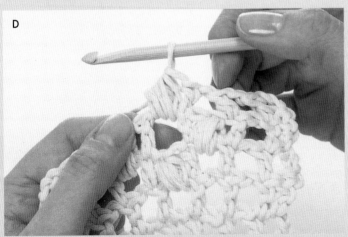

A

B

## CROSSED TREBLE CROCHET (ctr)

There are various crochet stitch patterns that involve crossing one stitch over another. The one shown here, which uses trebles, is one of the simplest. It produces a slightly open fabric with an attractive texture.

1   * Miss the next stitch on the previous row; yarn round hook and work 1 treble into the following stitch (fig. A).

2   Work 1 treble into the missed stitch. Repeat from * to end (fig. B). The sample (fig. C) shows a fabric made of crossed trebles.

C

# RINGS

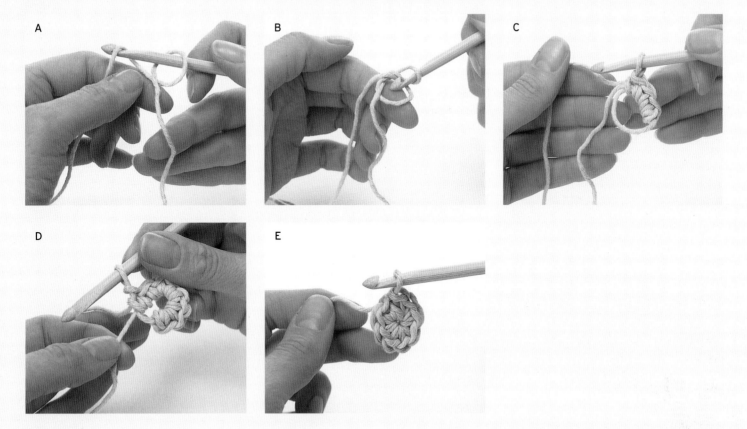

A    B    C

D    E

## Closed circle

This method of making a ring is used where you do not want a hole at the centre of the work. Practise it using a soft wool yarn, such as double knitting, which is easy to manage.

1   Loop the yarn around the hook as shown, with the tail hanging free in front of the loop, and take the working yarn round the hook (fig. A).

2   Draw the yarn through the ring (fig. B). When doing this you will need to hold the ring quite firmly with your left thumb and index finger to keep it open and prevent it from collapsing.

3   Still holding the ring firmly (the third finger of your right hand can help with this), work a double crochet over the ring. Note that you will be working over the ring and the tail end of yarn at this point.

4   Continue working double crochet into the ring (fig. C). When you have nearly the required number of stitches, pull gently on the tail end of yarn to close the ring (fig. D).

5   Work the last two or three stitches, then join the last double crochet to the first one with a slip stitch (fig. E). Continue with the second round as instructed in the pattern.

## Open circle

This is an easy ring to make. It is worked over a circle of chain stitches; the fewer the stitches, the smaller the hole

1   Work 5 chain - or the number specified in the pattern and close the ring with a slip stitch (figs a and b).

2   Work the specified number of stitches (here double crochet) into the ring (fig. C).

3   Close the first round by working a slip stitch into the first stitch. Then continue with the second round as instructed in the pattern (fig. D).

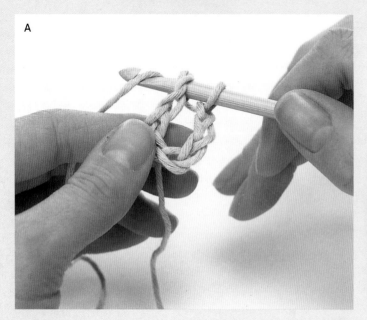

A

B

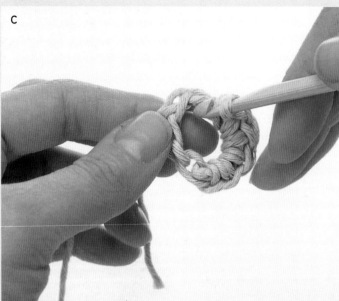

C

D

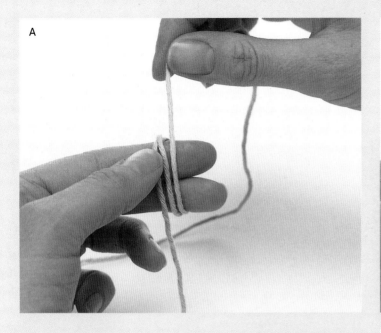

A

B

## Finger method

This method produces an effect similar to the open circle but is preferred where a relatively thick ring is desired at the centre.

1   Wind the yarn several times around your first two fingers as shown, leaving the tail of the yarn hanging down in front (fig. A).

2   Remove the yarn ring from your fingers and hold it in your right hand while tensioning the ball end of yarn as usual over your left.

3   Holding the ring with your left thumb and index finger, insert the hook through it; yarn round hook and pull it through the ring. You now have one loop on the hook.

4   Yarn round hook (fig. B) and pull it through this loop.

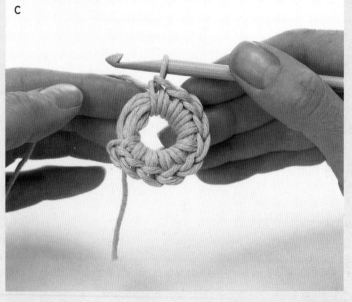

C

5   * Insert the hook through the ring. Yarn round hook and pull a loop through the ring (2 loops on hook). Yarn round hook and pull through both loops. One double crochet completed.

6   Repeat from * (fig. C)until ring is covered with double crochet. Trim excess tail just before last stitch; or leave it if required to sew the motif to the main fabric. Close with a slip stitch.

NOTE To make a smaller ring, simply wrap the yarn over one finger only.

# MAKING BOBBLES

Many stitch patterns incorporate bobbles, which produce a richly textured fabric. Bobbles are best worked on the wrong side and pushed to the front of your work. You can use any number of stitches in a cluster. Here is one popular way of making a 5-treble bobble.

1   * Yrh and insert the hook into the next stitch. Yrh again and draw a loop up (3 lps), yrh and draw through first 2 lps (2 lps).

2   Yrh again (fig. A). Inserting the hook into the same place, repeat the treble st in step 1, four times until you have 6 loops on the hook (fig. B).

3   Yrh and draw yarn through all of the loops (fig. C). Repeat from * for each bobble. Sample (fig. D) shows an all-over bobble pattern. Smaller sts between will make the bobbles more pronounced.

A

B

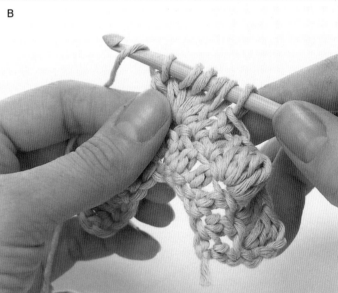

C

D

A

B

C

D

## SPIKE STITCH

A huge variety of multicolour effects can be produced with spike stitches. This is not a difficult technique, but achieving the right tension is crucial; with each stitch the yarn must be brought up to the new working row, without puckering the work. The more rows down the fabric that you work, the more care you must take to keep the fabric flat.

The sample shown includes rows of encroaching spikes, but the basic technique being worked is very simple: each stitch is worked over two previous rows of double crochet.

1  * Insert the hook into the stitch 2 rows down and directly below the stitch to be worked (fig. A).

2  Yarn round the hook and pull a loop through the fabric, drawing it up to the level of the working row (fig. B).

3  Yarn round hook and draw the yarn through the 2 loops on the hook – spike stitch made (fig. C). Repeat from * to the end. The sample shows different length spike sts in contrasting colours (fig. D).

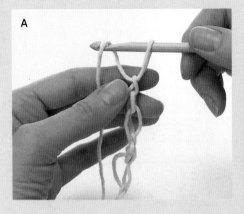

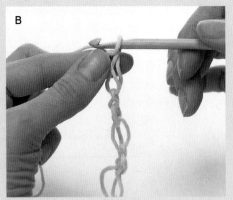

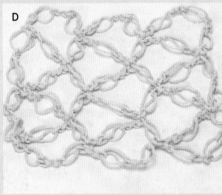

## SOLOMON'S KNOT (sk)

Although it's rather tricky to master, Solomon's knot is well worth the effort. It produces a wonderfully lacy mesh, suitable for all sorts of things, from scarves to string bags and curtains.

### First row
Begin, as usual, with a slip knot on the hook (several knots have previously been worked in this sample)

1   Make 1 chain and draw it up to the required length (typically about 2cm/¾in). * Yrh (fig. A) and draw it through long loop. This produces an extra, long strand behind the long loop.

3   Holding the back strand away from the loop with your left thumb and index finger, insert the hook underneath it (fig. B).

4   Yrh and draw it through the strand - 2 loops on hook (fig. C). Yrh and draw through both loops - Solomon's knot made. Repeat from * until you have the required (even) number of knots.

### Second row
1   Miss the next 3 knots from the hook and work a double crochet into the centre of the next knot.

2   * Extend the loop on the hook and make 2 Solomon's knots, each about half as long again as those in the first row.

3   Miss the next knot in the base row, and work a double crochet into the centre of the next knot. Repeat to the end of the row.

### Third row
1   Make 3 knots. Work a double crochet into the centre of the next free knot of the previous row.

2   * Make 2 knots. Work a double crochet into the centre of the next free knot of the previous row. Repeat from * to the end of the row.

Repeating the third row forms the pattern in fig. D.

# INTARSIA

 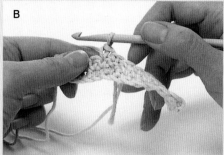 

Also called jacquard crochet, intarsia is a method of producing a multi-coloured fabric in which colours are changed within a row or round. If only two colours are being used, and are changed at frequent intervals (as in narrow vertical stripes), the colour not in use at any given time may be carried along the back of the work and simply crocheted over using the working yarn. This will, however, produce a denser fabric.

To prevent the old colour from encroaching on the new one, it's important to change to the new one when completing the stitch just before the actual colour change. For example:

## Changing colour in double crochet

1 Insert the hook into the last stitch before the colour change, take the yarn round hook and pull through (2 loops on hook).
2 Holding the old colour out of the way with your working hand, pick up the new colour and take it round the hook (fig. A); pull it through both loops to complete the stitch and colour change.
3 Continue working with the new colour, at the same time carrying the old colour along the row (fig. B). On both right-side and wrong-side rows, take the hook under the unused colour before working the stitch in the colour being used. The sample (fig. C) shows a finished piece of intarsia.

NOTE When you have changed to the new colour, you will need to pull the old yarn slightly to tighten the stitch. Avoid pulling it taut when carrying it across the back; otherwise the work will pucker.

## Changing colour in treble

1 Take the yarn round the hook and insert the hook into the last stitch before the colour change. Yarn round hook and pull a loop through (3 loops on hook).
2 Yarn round hook and pull a loop through first 2 loops on hook.
3 Holding the old colour out of the way with your working hand, pick up the new colour and pull it through the last 2 loops to complete the treble. The colour change is completed. Carry the old yarn along the work as described for double crochet.

## Working with separate lengths of yarn

It is necessary to use separate balls of yarn: where several colours are being used; where the change of colour is widely spaced; where there is a possibility of unused colours showing through on the right side; or where a denser fabric is undesirable. To prevent a tangle of yarns, it's advisable to wind lengths of the different colours onto plastic bobbins (available from needlecraft shops).

## Crossing the yarns

It is most important that when changing from one colour to another, you cross the yarns over each other on the wrong side; otherwise a hole will result along the colour change.

1 Change colours as described above, but leave the first one (called A) hanging loose. On the next WS row, when you reach the last stitch before changing back to yarn A, work this stitch in yarn B but do not complete it.
2 Allow yarn B to fall down along the wrong side of the work, and bring yarn A under yarn B and over it.
3 Complete the stitch using yarn A. The two yarns have been crossed.

On the following RS row complete the last stitch before the colour change in yarn B, first letting yarn A drop down on the wrong side and bringing yarn B under, then over it. After several rows, you will see that the yarns are twisted around each other, as a result of being crossed on each row.

When first introducing a new yarn simply knot them together loosely, and sew the ends in later. Whichever method you are using, you will have some loose ends on the wrong side. When the crochet is finished, use a tapestry needle to darn these in neatly.

# EDGINGS AND EMBELLISHMENTS

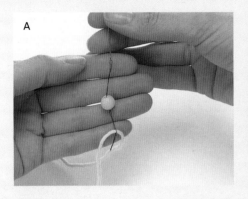

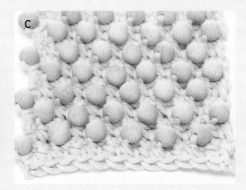

## WORKING WITH BEADS (ABOVE)

The addition of beads to a crocheted fabric will add texture and – in some cases – glamour. The best fabric for bead work is double crochet, which is solid enough to prevent the beads from slipping through to the wrong side and strong enough to bear their weight.

1   Thread a sewing needle with a short length of thread, double it and knot the ends. Slip one end of the yarn through the loop, and thread the required number of beads onto the yarn (fig. A).

2   Add the beads while working a wrong-side row. At the point for adding each bead, insert the hook into the next stitch, yrh (fig. B) and draw loop through (2 loops on hook).

3   Push a bead up close to the hook. Yrh and draw through both loops, completing a double crochet. Tighten the stitch if necessary to ensure that bead sits on the other (right) side of the fabric (fig. C).

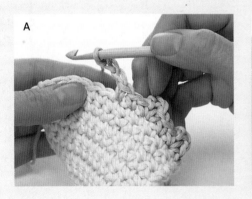

## PICOT EDGING (ABOVE)

Picots are neat little points, made of short lengths of chain forming a loop. They have a variety of uses. Sometimes they form part of a lacy stitch pattern, but more often they're used in edgings. The method described below produces a simple edging in which picots alternate with double crochet.
Fasten the yarn at one corner of the fabric.

1   Work 1 dc into first stitch. * Work 3 chain stitches (fig. A).

3   Slip stitch into same stitch – picot made (fig. B).

4   Work 1 double crochet into next two stitches. Repeat from * to end. If desired, the picots can be spaced out along the edge, with more double crochets worked in between them. Sample, fig. C, shows the completed picot edging.

## OPEN PICOT EDGING (ABOVE)

Open picots produce a lacier edging than normal picots. In the example shown here, they are joined to every alternate stitch of the main fabric.
Fasten the yarn at one corner.

1 * Work 4 (or more) chain stitches (fig. A).

2 Miss 1 stitch, 1 dc into next stitch (fig. B). Repeat from * to end. Sample, fig. C, shows completed open picot edging.

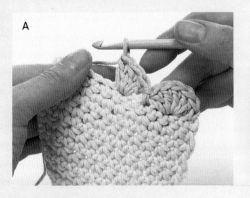

## SHELL EDGING (ABOVE)

This scalloped edging is particularly attractive when worked in a contrasting colour, though it can equally well be worked in the same colour. The fabric edge should consist of a multiple of 4 stitches, plus 1 extra stitch at the end. Begin by fastening the yarn to the first stitch at the edge of the fabric.

1 * Miss the next stitch and work 5 trebles into the following stitch (fig. A shows 3 trebles worked).

2 Miss the next stitch and work 1 dc into the following stitch (fig. B). Repeat from * along the edge, ending with a dc into the last stitch. The sample, fig. C, shows the shell edging completed.

If you need to continue the edging along the adjacent vertical edge, keep the spacing the same. Work a row of double crochet, in the same yarn as the main fabric, to provide a good foundation for the shell edging.

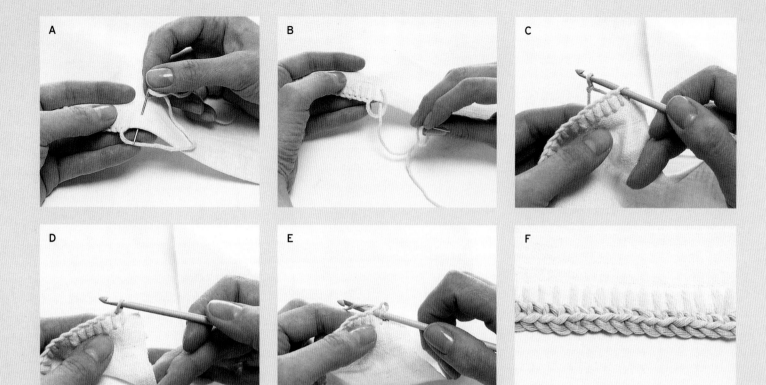

## BLANKET STITCH WITH DOUBLE CROCHET EDGING

This method – which can be varied by means of different crochet stitches – is used where you wish to apply a crochet edging to a piece of woven fabric. You will need a sharp-pointed embroidery needle, such as a chenille needle, with an eye large enough for your chosen yarn or thread. It's a good idea to practise this technique on a spare piece of fabric, in order to get the spacing correct.

1    Fasten the yarn on the wrong side of the fabric, close to edge. With the right side of the fabric facing you, insert the needle a short distance to the right, at the desired height of the stitch, and bring it up over the thread at the lower edge (fig. A). Pull the thread through gently, so that the loop sits on the edge of the fabric.

2    Continue in this way, spacing the stitches evenly along the fabric edge (fig. B). Do not pull the thread too tightly. When the stitching is complete, fasten off the thread on the wrong side.

3    Insert the crochet hook through the first blanket stitch as shown and place a slip knot on it (fig. C).

4    Draw the loop through the edge of the blanket stitch (fig. D).

5    * Insert the hook into the next blanket stitch; yarn round hook and draw a loop through (fig. E).

6    Yarn round hook and through both loops on hook – one double crochet completed. Repeat from * to the end of the row. Fasten off. The sample, fig f, shows the completed edging.

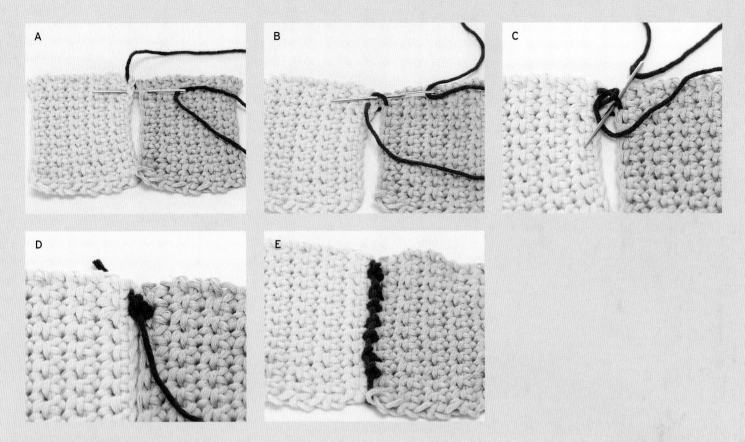

## DOUBLE KNOT STITCH

This is a decorative way of joining two pieces of crochet, especially suitable for a blanket or other household accessory. Work the stitching with a blunt tapestry needle, so as not to split the embroidered or crocheted stitches.

1   Place the motifs side by side, with right sides facing upwards.

2   Fasten the embroidery thread with a couple of backstitches on the wrong side of the left-hand piece and bring it through to the right side of the fabric, close to the corner.

3   * Insert the needle in the right-hand piece, a short distance down, and bring it up in the left-hand piece, exactly opposite (fig. A). Pull the thread through. This forms a small diagonal stitch linking the two pieces.

4   Slip the needle under this stitch from right to left, without entering the crochet fabric (fig. B). Pull the thread through, but not too tightly, to form the first part of the knot.

5   Loop the thread anti-clockwise below the stitch and take the needle under the stitch again, then over the loop (fig. C). Pull gently to complete the knot (fig. D). Repeat steps from * to the end. The sample, fig. E, shows a completed row of double knot stitch.

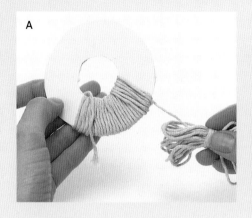

A

B

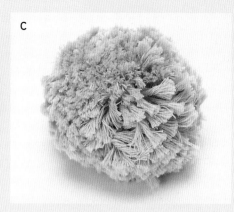

C

## POMPOMS

You can buy forms for making pompoms at needlecraft shops. Alternatively, you can use circles cut from cardboard. Use an object of the required diameter (such as a cosmetics jar) as a template. Draw around it twice on a piece of cardboard and cut out the two circles. In the centre of one circle, draw a smaller circle, about one-third to one-half the diameter of the outer circle. The thicker the yarn, the larger the inner circle should be. Measure inwards at several points to make sure the circle is centred. Cut out the inner circle. Place the completed circle over the other circle and trace the inner circle. Cut this out.

1   Place the two rings together and wind yarn over them (fig. A) until the centre hole is nearly full.

2   Cut the yarn around the edge of the two rings.

3   Wind a length of yarn between the cardboard circles (fig. B). Tie the yarn tightly around the cut threads, then remove the rings. Leave the long ends for attaching the pompom.

4   Fluff out the threads to finish the pompom (fig. C). If any threads stick out, trim the ends.

## CURLICUE TASSEL

Begin by making the required length of chain. This will usually be stated in the pattern. If not, or if you are designing your own curlicue tassel, experiment to find a suitable length.

1   Into the 2nd chain from the hook work 1 double crochet, 1 half-treble and 1 treble.

2   * Into the next chain work at least 4 trebles. Repeat from * along the length of the chain. Use the working yarn to fasten the curlicue to the edge of the fabric (see fig. A) with a slip stitch or double crochet, then use a tapestry needle to darn the ends into the tassel or the edge of the fabric.

Note that the more trebles you work into the chain, the more the tassel will curl.

A

# MAKING UP

## BLOCKING

To block a piece of crocheted fabric, pin it out to the correct size and shape, then press or damp-finish it. The blocked pieces are then sewn together. Blocking gives a smooth finish and proper shape to the crocheted fabric, stretching edges that are pulling, sharpening points and corners and drawing buttonhole slits together.

Blocking is done on a blocking pad laid on a firm, flat surface, such as an ironing board, kitchen table or floor. The blocking pad should be fairly thick; a large folded clean towel or an old blanket covered with a white cloth will suffice. Pins should be rustless and have glass or other highly visible heads. Err on the side of generosity when using the pins.

Read the ball band for the yarn to check the pressing instructions. If using more than one yarn, follow the gentlest method of pressing or use the damp-finishing method, described below. Do not press highly textured stitch patterns. Damp finishing is recommended for the novice or the nervous.

### Pinning out

With the wrong side of the crochet uppermost, pin out each piece along the edges to size and shape, making sure that the rows and the columns of stitches are straight. The pins should be at right angles to the fabric.

### Pressing

1   Cover the crocheted piece with a white cloth. As a general rule, use a dry cloth for synthetics and a damp cloth for natural fibres, both with a dry iron. Be guided by the pressing instructions on the ball band.

2   Heat the iron to the correct temperature, as stated on the ball band.

3   Put the iron on the cloth and immediately lift it up again. Repeat all over the crocheted piece. Never use an ironing motion.

4   Leave the cloth in place until cool and/or dry.

### Damp finishing

1   Fill a spray bottle with cold water and lightly spray the crocheted piece until damp.

2   Cover with a clean white cloth and pat gently to absorb excess water.

3   Remove the cloth and allow the crocheted piece to dry naturally.

## SEAMS

Before joining pieces of crochet, darn in any loose ends on the wrong side of the work.

There are various ways of joining the pieces. They may be placed wrong side up on a flat surface and sewn together edge to edge, using whip stitch and working the stitches through one loop only of each edge. Or they can be placed together with right sides facing and joined with crochet, using slip stitches. If the edges are uneven and a strong join is required, you can sew them, right sides together, with backstitch, using a tapestry needle. For a decorative effect, you can place them together with wrong sides facing and work double crochet over the two edges, using a contrasting colour. Or join the seams with Double Knot Stitch.

# Suppliers

**Loop**
41 Cross Street, Islington,
London N1 2BB, UK
Tel: +44 (0)20 7288 1160
www.loop.gb.com
*All of the yarns and haberdashery
shown in this book are available
at Loop and from Loop's online
shop. We ship worldwide.*

## YARN
*Contact the companies below
for your nearest supplier.*

**Be Sweet**
1315 Bridgeway, Sausalito,
CA 94965, USA
Tel: +1 415 331 9676
www.besweetproducts.com

**Blue Sky Alpacas**
PO Box 88, Cedar,
MN 55011, USA
Tel: +1 888 460 8862
www.blueskyalpacas.com

**Designer Yarns**
Unit 8-10 Newbridge Industrial
Estate, Pitt Street, Keighley, West
Yorkshire BD21 4PQ, UK
Tel: +44 (0)1535 664 222
www.designeryarns.uk.com
*Debbie Bliss and Louisa Harding
yarns, among others.*

**ggh**
Mühlenstraße 74, 25421
Pinneberg, Germany
Tel: +49 (0)4101 208 484
www.ggh-garn.de

**Jade Sapphire**
148 Germonds Road, West Nyack,
NY 10994, USA
Tel: +1 866 857 3897
www.jadesapphire.com

**Lana Grossa**
Heritage Stitchcraft,
Redrook Lane, Rugeley,
Staffordshire, WS15 1QU, UK
Tel: +44 (0)1889 585 666
www.lanagrossa.com

**pear tree**
PO Box 463, Torquay, Victoria,
Australia 3228
Tel: +61 03 5261 6375
www.peartreeproducts.com

**Rowan**
Green Lane Mill, Holmfirth
HD9 2DX, UK
Tel: +44 (0)1484 681 881
www.knitrowan.com
*Rowan and Jaeger yarns.*

**Texere Yarns**
College Mill, Barkerend Road,
Bradford, West Yorkshire
BD1 4AU, UK
Tel: +44 (0)1274 722 191
www.texere.co.uk
*Yarns and supplies for knitting,
sewing, felt-making and weaving.*

## FABRICS
*In addition to using fabric to line
bags or purses, or as an edging
for a blanket or throw, you can
also crochet with it. Cut or rip the
fabric into narrow strips and tie
these into a ball of 'yarn' to work
with. It takes a surprisingly large
number of strips to make up
enough to work with, so buy more
fabric than you think you will
need. If your project requires only
a small amount of fabric, consider
using vintage clothes or curtains.
Fabric strips and ribbons also
look lovely threaded through
crocheted pieces, especially
the more open crochet stitches.*

*A huge variety of fabric is
available from specialist
independent fabric shops and
department stores, while lovely
vintage fabrics may be found
at flea markets, secondhand
shops, textile fairs and on the
Internet. Here are a few of my
favourite sources:*

**Alfies Antiques Market**
13-25 Church Street, London NW8
8DT, UK
Tel: +44 (0)20 7723 6066
www.alfiesantiques.com
*Among a lot of other wonderful
things, this antiques emporium
has dealers specializing in textiles,
lace and linen.*

**Cloth House**
47 Berwick Street, Soho, London
W1F 8SJ, UK
Tel: +44 (0)20 7437 5155
www.clothhouse.com
*A wonderful fabric shop
specializing in natural fabrics
and vintage trimmings. There
is another branch at number 98,
which stocks silk, wool, felt, jersey,
embroidered fabric, innovative
synthetic fabric and leather.*

**Liberty**
Regent Street, London
W1B 5AH, UK
Tel: +44 (0)20 7734 1234
www.liberty.co.uk
*First opened in 1875, selling fabric
and objets d'art from Japan and
the East, it still has an amazing
array of the iconic Liberty fabrics.*

**reprodepot.com**
www.reprodepot.com
*A nice website that sells
reproductions of vintage fabric.*

## RIBBON AND TRIMS
**Temptation Alley**
359/361 Portobello Road, London
W10 5SA, UK
Tel: +44 (0)20 8964 2004
www.temptationalley.com
*A helpful, friendly shop offering
an amazing selection of very
reasonably priced ribbons, trims,
tassels, beads, feathers, sequins
and lace. They ship worldwide.*

**V V Rouleaux**
102 Marylebone Lane, London
W1U 2QD, UK
Tel: +44 (0)20 7224 5179
www.vvrouleaux.com
*Fantastic selection of ribbons and
trims. There are also shops in Sloane
Square, Glasgow and Newcastle.*

**Turkish 'Oya' lace flowers**
Available from Loop.
*The history of the decorative
edging known in Europe as
'Turkish lace' dates back to the
8th century BC. These needle-lace
flowers are made in villages
across Turkey, traditionally by
farming women, who used them
to decorate their scarves. They
are charming threaded together
in clusters as an embellishment
or trim.*

## BUTTONS

*Besides being functional, buttons can be used as embellishments. You can use one stunning huge one with other smaller elements (such as small buttons, tiny pompoms or beads), or use beautiful vintage buttons in clusters or scattered along an edge. For unusual or vintage examples, try vintage-textile fairs, which are usually advertised in local papers or craft and textile magazines such as Crafts and Selvedge. In London, Portobello Market is good for finds, as well as the Vintage Textile Fair at Hammersmith Town Hall a few times a year. You can also mooch around flea markets, jumble sales and secondhand shops. It's often worth looking at secondhand clothing to see if the buttons are interesting – you can cut them off and use them for your new piece. Ebay is also a good source.*

### The Button Queen
19 Marylebone Lane, London
W1V 2NF, UK
Tel: +44 (0)20 7935 1505
www.thebuttonqueen.co.uk

### Tender Buttons
143 E 62nd Street, New York, NY 10021, USA
Tel: +1 212 758 7004
*They don't have an online shop, but there is no way I could leave out this gem of a shop. It is, quite simply, the best button shop I have ever been to in the world. If you are ever anywhere near NYC, make a beeline for it.*

## BEADS

*Check the Internet, as there are a lot of online shops that sell all kinds of beads.*

### Creative Beadcraft
20 Beak Street, London
W1F 9RE, UK
Tel: +44 (0)20 7629 9964
www.creativebeadcraft.co.uk
*Beads, sequins and trims.*

## PURSE CLASPS AND BAG HANDLES AND FRAMES

### Lacis
3163 Adeline Street, Berkeley, CA 94703, USA
Tel: +1 510 843 7178
www.lacis.com
*Fabulous selection of the most exquisite bag and purse frames and handles. They have vintage Lucite and other beauties.*

### U-Handbag
150 McLeod Road, London
SE2 0BS, UK
Tel: +44 (0)20 8310 3612
www.U-handbag.com
*A very useful website selling bamboo, wood, metal and plastic handles of all shapes and sizes. They also have a great selection of both bag and purse frames.*

## CUSHIONS

### Allshapes Cushions Ltd
Unit 29, Vernon Building, Westbourne Street, High Wycombe, Bucks HP11 2PX, UK
Tel: +44 (0)1494 465 581
www.allshapes.co.uk
*This company will make pads to any size and are very reliable; they also have a helpful website.*

## TENT SUPPLIES

### Tentsmiths
Box 1748, Conway, NH 03818, USA
Tel: +1 (603) 447 2344
www.tentsmiths.com
*Tents, accessories and rope. Leigh Radford found this company while researching for her Papillon Canopy.*

## PROP CREDITS

The publisher and author would also like to thank the following individuals and companies for kindly lending props for the photoshoot:

### Julie Arkell 'Trolley Creature'
(as seen on page 99).
Wide selection available at Loop and at Flow Gallery, 1–5 Needham Road, London W11 2RP, UK
Tel: +44 (0)20 7243 0782
www.flowgallery.co.uk

### Caravan
11 Lamb Street, Old Spitalfields Market, London E1 6EA, UK
Tel:+ 44 (0)20 7247 6467
www.caravanstyle.com
*An eclectic and unusual mix for the home and to wear. Caravan offers a wide range of new and old pieces. Stock includes handknitted toys for cats, vintage teapots, brightly coloured industrial-style lighting and skirts crafted from vintage floral fabrics.*

### Gladys Carvell cardigan by Keep & Share
(as seen on page 115).
Available at Loop and at Keep & Share, Lugwardine Court, Lugwardine, Hereford HR1 4AE, UK
Tel: +44 (0)1432 851 162
www.keepandshare.co.uk

## Crochet hooks

Selection of assorted crochet hooks used and featured throughout – Clover Soft-Touch and Bamboo, Balene and Susan Bates, all available at Loop or your nearest stockist.

### Hannah Lamb
16a Ashfield Terrace, Bingley, West Yorkshire BD16 1EQ, UK
Tel: +44 (0)1274 781346
www.hannahlamb.co.uk
*Carefully detailed, beautifully handmade accessories. Hannah creates practical pieces for the home and to wear, from a carefully planned combination of nostalgic ephemera.*

### Life's a Picnic
Contact Elly and Evie Pace
Tel: +44 (0)20 7790 0335/
+44 (0)7966 149533
www.lifesapicnic.co.uk
*Luncheon hampers that are classy, fun and totally individual. Willow picnic hampers lined with vintage fabrics and fully fitted with vintage tableware and linen.*

### Amy Ruppel paintings
(as seen on pages 7 and 52).
Available at Loop and at www.amyruppel.com
*These are made by the lovely Amy Ruppel in Portland, Oregon, by mixing pigment with encaustic resin and beeswax applied to wood. They are the only thing I sell at Loop that has absolutely nothing to do with knitting or crochet, but they make me happy. Some people say that the nests remind them of balls of yarn, so there you go.*

# Designers' Biographies

**BEE CLINCH** has always been fascinated by the wonder of handmade objects – from a rag rug, to a swatch of sixties floral fabric, to a seventies mohair sweater. As she grew up, first in California and then in England, Bee became obsessed with the variety of textures and colours of yarn and how it can be transformed into something wonderful by crochet.

Bee is determined to show that everyone can enjoy the versatility of crochet, and through her design work and teaching, she is able to pursue her love for the craft and explore this potentially endless expression of creativity.
**www.bee-at-home.co.uk**

**KRISTEEN GRIFFIN-GRIMES** is a designer based in Washington State and creator of French Girl's hallmark style of knit and crochet patterns: ethereal, draped garments superbly fitting to the feminine form. French Girl patterns are constructed in a unique manner, the garments fashioned in one piece from start to finish. Using her seamstress and costuming background, Kristeen begins her design process almost architecturally, to deconstruct her envisioned garment and reconstruct it again in a more organic way, either from the top down, from the hem up, or from the back out.

The designer's aesthetic is rooted in her early years as a 'nature girl' on her family's oyster farm on the rural Pacific Northwest coast.
**www.frenchgirlknits.com**

**BOBBI INTVELD** was born and raised in Minnesota, USA. She began working in her grandmothers yarn shop in White Bear Lake at the age of 12, and very soon learnt to knit, crochet and design her own patterns.

Bobbi is now an enthusiastic designer, who has had both knit and crochet patterns published. She also teaches, aiming to pass on her love for these crafts to others.

**KATE JENKINS** worked as a knitwear consultant for various fashion houses, including Marc Jacobs and Donna Karan, before founding her own company, Cardigan, in 2003. With a strong emphasis on colour and innovative quirky details, Cardigan has become synonymous with the creation of beautiful knitted and crocheted accessories. Cardigan's philosophy is that anything can be knitted as long as the products are made with love.

2006 saw the opening of Cardigan's first studio shop in Brighton, where customers can view the entire Cardigan collection and see the beautiful studio where the designs are created.
**www.cardigan.ltd.uk**

**CLAIRE MONTGOMERIE** has an MA in Constructed Textiles from the Royal College of Art, London. She has a wealth of experience in the craft and textile industries and runs a successful online business selling her quirky knitted wares. Claire teaches knitting classes at Loop, children's textile courses at the artsdepot, London, and textile jewellery courses at West Dean College, Sussex.

Claire is the author of *Easy Baby Knits* and the co-author of *London Crochet*. She has also contributed designs to *Hookorama*, *Instant Expert Crochet* and Loop: *Pretty Knits*.
**www.clairemontgomerie.com**

**ALICIA PAULSON** is a designer of handmade products and crochet-wear, who lives in Portland, Oregon, in a house filled with pets, flowers and far too much yarn. She writes daily on her blog (aliciapaulson.com) about life, love, and all things crafty, and is working on a book of memory-inspired sewing projects. Her small collection of one-of-a-kind handmade accessories and crochet patterns is available from her website.
**www.rosylittlethings.com**.

**LEIGH RADFORD** is an award-winning author, designer and teacher living in the Pacific Northwest. Her books include the highly popular *AlterKnits: Imaginative Projects and Creativity Exercises* and *One Skein: 30 Quick Projects to Knit & Crochet*.

In 2006 Leigh created Silk Gelato, offering knitters a fibre with enhanced texture and rich colour for her unique pattern designs. Her enterprising efforts have resulted in a highly successful business collaboration with Lantern Moon, producers of Silk Gelato.

Leigh is in demand for her innovative classes and workshops. She enjoys teaching others the value of being creative and is inspired by the expression of original ideas that lend a fresh perspective to knitting and crochet.
**www.leighradford.com**

**KATE SAMPHIER** was inspired by traditional knitting in Scotland and her collections embrace Scottish knitwear manufacture, challenging tradition with an eclectic use of colour, texture and pattern.

After studying textiles in the Scottish Borders, Kate worked for a local woollen spinner for five years as a yarn and knit-fabric designer. Drawn to the raw material and colours that she worked with, Kate began to create her own knitted accessories to illustrate the versatility of the company's yarn ranges.

In Spring 2000 Kate set up her design studio and workshop. The following year her first collection of knitted accessories was launched. Featured in magazines such as *Easy Living*, *Homes and Gardens*, *Junior* and *Selvedge*, Kate's designs are for women with an eye for beauty and a quirky sense of style.
**www.katesamphier.co.uk**

**EMMA SEDDON** was taught to knit by her grandmother, and has never looked back. She trained at Central St Martins School of Art, where she did a Knitted Textiles degree. Working for the next 12 years on a variety of different textiles products, she spent most of her free time knitting, crocheting and sewing, taking the odd spare moment to peruse charity shops for patterns and balls of yarn.

In 2004 she became freelance, to pursue her first loves of knitting and crochet, and to inspire others to do the same, through teaching. She works with Rowan as a freelance design consultant, teaches at local colleges and works on a wide range of design projects.

**NICKI TRENCH** founded Laughing Hens, a UK mail-order knitting website, which has captured a new wave of interest in knitting as a modern creative hobby for women. Nicki has written two books, *The Cool Girl's Guide to Knitting* and *The Cool Girl's Guide to Crochet*, and is currently writing a third, *The Cool Girl's Guide to Sewing*.

Nicki's inspiration has always been colour and texture, and she loves vintage designs in fabric and textile. The flowers, dots and stripes represented in her designs draw from 1950s retro and 1960s colour. Her background in wedding-cake design is reflected in her handknitting and crochet – opulent big roses and pretty, delicate flowers and leaves in yummy coloured yarns that look good enough to eat.
**www.laughinghens.com**

**JUJU VAIL** came to the UK in 1990 to study for an MA in Textile Design at St Martins, after studying fashion and knitwear design in Montreal. Since graduating, she has taught and written books and articles on many creative practices. These include quilting, sewing, beading, knitting, crochet, painting and rug making.

Juju has a whim of iron and chronicles her creative passions on her blog. Her latest book is *Creative Beadwork*.
**www.jujulovespolkadots.typepad.com**

# Acknowledgements

This book was blessed with a wonderful team of talented people, who were all a joy to work with. It was so important to me that as well as being chock-full of really great patterns, the book would have a cosy, beautiful warmth. All of the people involved helped realize that dream for me and I thank them all.

First and foremost I wish to express my thanks to all the talented designers, both in the UK and America, who have contributed their creativity and sensibility to this project. That they took time out of their already very hectic lives has truly touched me. Each of them is taking crochet in a wonderful direction and inspiring a new generation of people to take up the craft, by making it inspiring and exciting.

Thanks to Kristin Perers. Her incredible eye and artisan spirit informs all of the images. In addition to taking the beautiful photographs, she tweaked and fiddled until everything was 'just so', and the care she took is obvious in every frame. Thank you, also, to Heather Lewin, Kristin's brilliant assistant.

A huge thank you to sweet Emily Chalmers. Her quirky sense of style is enchanting and I feel honoured to have had her work on this project. Like a magpie, she swoops on everyday things and finds some unique beauty in them. From cupcakes to dog trollies, she left no stone unturned.

Thanks to both Emily and Debi Treloar for the use of their charming homes that were like treasure troves, and to Bee Clinch for her peaceful 'country spread'.

Thanks to the lovely Lucy Chapman and Rosie Doren, who modelled the garments so professionally; and to Emma Seddon, who swatched everything for the techniques section.

Also, big thank you to Zia Mattocks, my commissioning editor, who, with her cool head, kept things ticking at all times. Thanks also to Barbara Zuñiga, our book designer, who, once again, I had the great fortune to have on this project. And, of course, to Jacqui Small, who thought of the book in the first place. Thank you for approaching Loop and believing in the book and making it happen.

Thanks to Blue Sky Alpacas, Designer Yarns for Debbie Bliss and Louisa Harding's yarns, ggh, Rowan, Jaeger, pear tree, Jade Sapphire, Lana Grossa and Be Sweet for their support and generosity (and for making such beautiful yarns!).

My heartfelt thanks to the incredible staff at Loop. I have been lucky enough, right from the beginning, to have warm, responsible, helpful people, who happen to be great at knitting and crochet as well. Thank you to Linda Marveng, Claire Montgomerie and Stefan Reekie. Your grace and enthusiasm for the craft have made the shop an everyday joy and the book possible. Also thanks to our talented teachers, whose patience, together with their passion for knitting and crochet, is truly inspiring: Bee Clinch, Emma Seddon, Juju Vail, Aneeta Patel, Laura Long, Julie Arkell, Jane Lithgow and, of course, Linda and Claire. Thank you to Emerald Mosley, my ever-faithful website designer, who makes it so beautiful.

And also, thank you to all Loop's customers – your enthusiasm for the craft keeps it all fresh and exciting, and is the reason we are here.

To Joy, who likes to mooch around the yarn fairs with me and makes samples for the shop, and my dad, Jack Silverberg – thank you both for all of the kind support you have given. And my brother, David, who sends me farflung messages from faraway places and a heads-up when he discovers anyone involved in textiles who he thinks might inspire me.

Thanks to my mom, Joan Podel, who dragged me around the museums and design fairs of NYC as a child, and gave me a passion for design and simple beauty through osmosis. Those yarns hanging in our bathroom for your weaving in the seventies must have seeped into my system. A heartfelt thanks for your unwavering enthusiasm for everything that I ever do, and for Loop.

I couldn't have done any of this book without the huge support on the home front from my dear husband, Steven, and our three beautiful children, Sonia, Niall and Jonah. They have been generous beyond belief and endlessly patient with me and the piles of yarns, hooks, needles, ribbons, buttons, stacks of papers, and scribbled notes and poloroids stuck on walls that have graced our home over the course of the year. I know you will secretly miss it all.